AN UNCOMMON ATLAS

Brimming with creative inspiration, how-to projects and useful information to enrich your everyday life, Quarto Knows is a favourite destination for those pursuing their interests and passions. Visit our site and dig deeper with our books into your area of interest: Quarto Creates, Quarto Cooks, Quarto Homes, Quarto Lives, Quarto Drives, Quarto Explores, Quarto Gifts, or Quarto Kids.

First published in 2017 by Aurum Press,
an imprint of The Quarto Group.
The Old Brewery, 6 Blundell Street,
London, N7 9BH,
United Kingdom
T (0)20 7700 6700
www.QuartoKnows.com

This revised and updated edition first published in 2019 by White Lion Publishing
Previously published as *New Views: The World Mapped Like Never Before*

ISBN 978 1 78131 899 7

10 9 8 7 6 5 4 3 2 1

Designed by Paileen Currie
Maps by Lovell Johns
Printed in Slovenia

AN
UNCOMMON
ATLAS

50 NEW VIEWS OF OUR
PHYSICAL, CULTURAL
AND POLITICAL WORLD

ALASTAIR BONNETT

WHITE LION
PUBLISHING

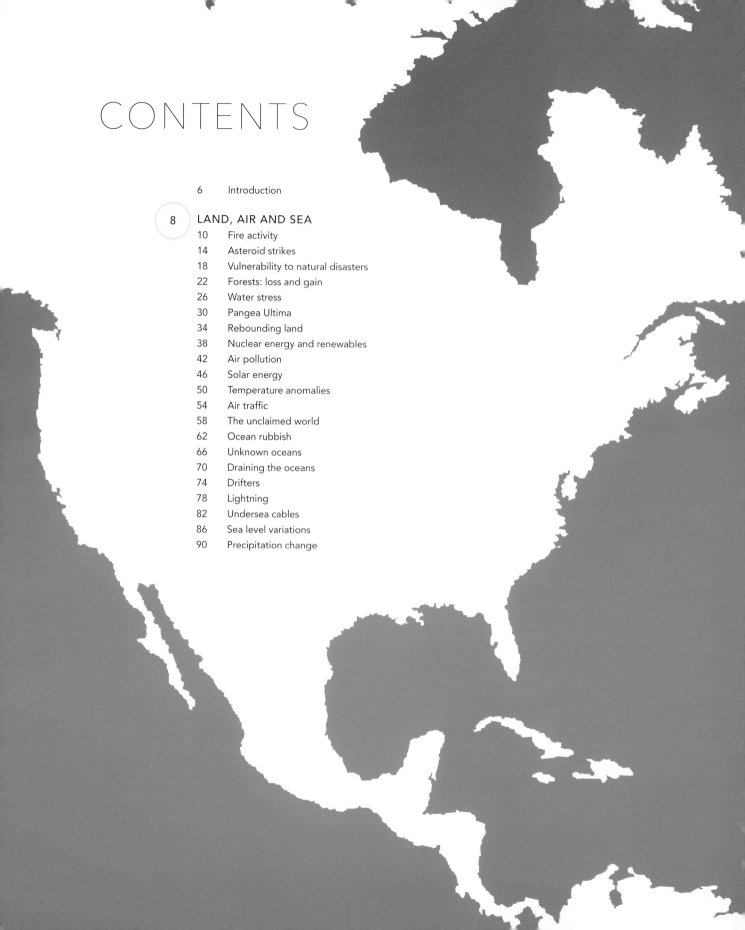

CONTENTS

6   Introduction

8   LAND, AIR AND SEA
10   Fire activity
14   Asteroid strikes
18   Vulnerability to natural disasters
22   Forests: loss and gain
26   Water stress
30   Pangea Ultima
34   Rebounding land
38   Nuclear energy and renewables
42   Air pollution
46   Solar energy
50   Temperature anomalies
54   Air traffic
58   The unclaimed world
62   Ocean rubbish
66   Unknown oceans
70   Draining the oceans
74   Drifters
78   Lightning
82   Undersea cables
86   Sea level variations
90   Precipitation change

94 **HUMAN AND ANIMAL**

96   Amphibian diversity
100   Ants
104   Bird diversity
108   Countries with the largest number of venomous animals
112   Neglected tropical diseases
116   Five per cent of the world's population
120   Ecological footprint per capita
124   Peacefulness
128   The Black Marble
132   Linguistic diversity
136   Total fertility rate
140   Religious diversity
144   Obesity
148   Happiness

152 **GLOBALISATION**

154   Twitter relationships
158   US fast-food franchises
162   Shipping routes
166   Energy flux
170   Number of migrants
174   Flow of people
178   People living in the US born outside the US
182   Remoteness from city
186   Critically endangered languages
190   World nut trade
194   Petrol prices
198   Edible insects
202   Guns
206   Problem drugs
210   Sugar consumption

214   Map Projections
218   Bibliography
220   Index
223   Credits
224   Acknowledgements

INTRODUCTION

Mapping the world has never been more exciting or more necessary. This book introduces fifty maps of a fast-changing planet; fifty new views that will surprise and provoke but also make us think about life on earth in fresh ways.

It is a roller-coaster ride, taking us from what might, at first glance, appear to be arcane topics – such as Edible insects and Lightning – to some of the biggest social issues of our day, such as Flow of people and Ecological footprint per capita. We'll find out why the geography of all these things, including tasty crickets and lightning bolts, matters.

Maps are increasingly at the centre of our culture. With so many people carrying devices that can map out the world in an instant, we've become a carto-centric civilisation. Our fifty maps are derived, in large measure, from our recent ability to harness mass data, be it on Bird diversity or levels of Peacefulness. The amazing world views that are being produced, by NASA satellites in particular, are revolutionising the way we see the earth. Over the last decade or so, we have gained access to pictures of the world of unprecedented quality, detail and comprehensiveness. From Fire activity to The Black Marble, the resulting maps are incredibly useful tools for anyone who needs to know where the biggest challenges we face are and, hence, where solutions should be targeted.

But they are also much more: they are beautiful, enthralling and thrilling.

These fifty maps distil innumerable terabytes of data but, more importantly, millions of hours of expertise. To take just one example, the map we present of the Unknown oceans is based on the most wide-ranging census of life the planet has ever seen, involving thousands of scientists and hundreds of expeditions, whose work led to the discovery of 6,000 new species. *An Uncommon Atlas* arises from and, I like to think, is a kind of tribute to these and similar endeavours.

There is grandeur to the world map. It can be a little too seductive. Finer and often very important details are lost, and we gain only a sweeping and large-scale view. But in a globally interconnected world, where we need to see the big picture, such an overview is ever more vital. World maps capture an issue immediately; almost at first glance one can grasp levels of Peacefulness or Water stress across the entire planet. On closer inspection, we begin to see connections between countries, regional patterns and similarities, which are key to a global understanding.

We have chosen these maps because each of them has something original and important to tell us. We have sought to capture a broad sweep of issues, some of which are purely social, like Guns, and some solely natural, like Rebounding land or Pangea Ultima. But we'll also see how often the world map connects the human and the natural; that the geography of many 'natural' phenomena, such as Bird diversity or Temperature anomalies, is being shaped by human activity.

Sometimes the link between nature and society comes most fully to life in maps covering topics that, perhaps, we never thought could be mapped. For example, our map of Petrol prices tells us as much about how governments like to manipulate the price of petrol as it does about which countries are sitting on oil wells. The world map of Ocean rubbish is a portrait both of our throwaway culture and the seas' natural circulatory systems.

'Anyone who opens an atlas wants everything at once, without limits – the whole world,' writes Judith Schalansky, author of *Atlas of Remote Islands*. 'Give me an atlas over a guidebook any day,' she says, for there is 'no more poetic book in the world.' *An Uncommon Atlas* is a book of hard facts and real data but, perhaps, it too has a touch of poetry. The ambition and the wonder of the map draw in our eye and feed our imagination.

LAND, AIR
AND SEA

FIRE ACTIVITY

0.0–0.4

0.4–0.467

0.467–0.533

0.533–0.6

0.6–0.667

0.667–0.733

0.733–0.8

0.8–0.867

0.867–0.933

0.933–1.0

Not considered

Derived from data on wildfires and burnable
plant cover

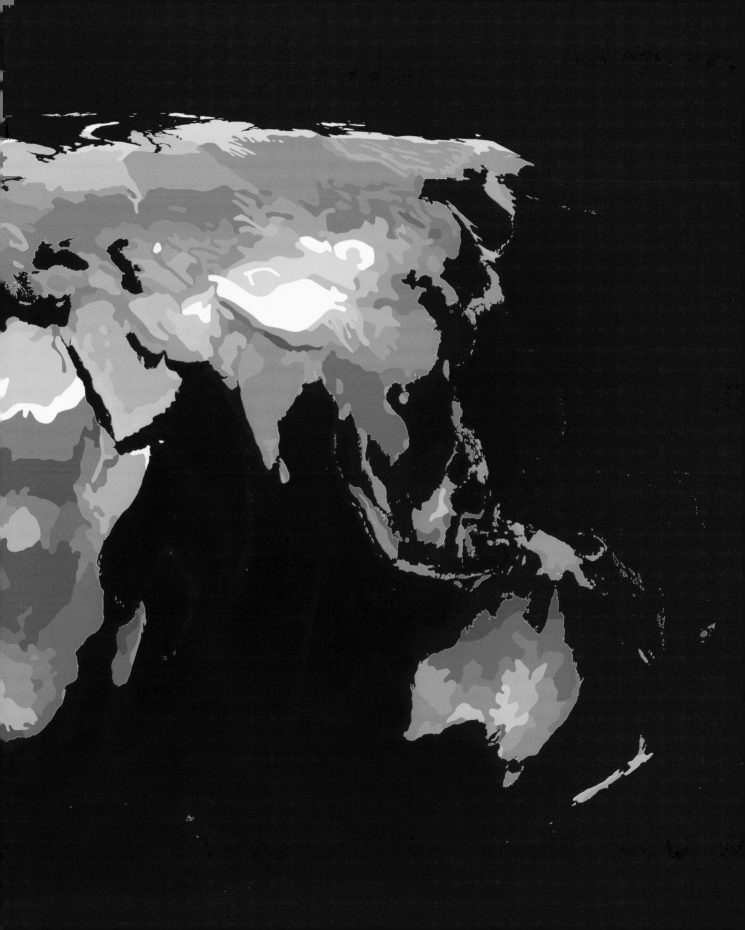

FIRE ACTIVITY

Fire is both a destructive and a creative force. It destroys vegetal growth and human and animal lives, but it can also be an important part of the ecosystem. This is a map of where fires are most likely to occur. It is an ecologically based map that combines satellite data on wildfires with data on burnable plant cover to create a fire activity index that ranges from 0 (least activity) to 1 (most activity). The result is a picture of which parts of the world are most prone to fire. The importance of the ecological dimension is that it allows us to see not just incidence but vulnerability. The maps show us that the hottest places on the planet, such as the Sahara, are less vulnerable to fire than much colder regions. This is because in a desert there is so little to burn. The Tropics are the places where you are most likely to come across a serious and devastating wildfire. From Central America and Amazonia across to Sub-Saharan Africa and on to Northern Australia, there is a ragged band of bright red, that is both hot and lush.

This map would not have been possible without data collected by NASA's Fire Information for Resource Management System. A NASA satellite continually collects snapshots of burning wildfires, and makes the resultant maps available within three hours of each overflight. This endlessly updated portrait of our burning planet means that wildfires can be tracked and identified more efficiently than ever before.

The smouldering band of fire shown across the map is not necessarily a destructive force. Juli Pausas, a plant ecologist at the Desertification Research Centre in Spain, who collected and compiled the data for this map, explains that 'some plants flower only after a fire, and some develop thicker barks to survive'. It turns out that 'fires are very old in our ecosystems'. For Pausas, 'a world without fires is like a sphere without roundness; that is, we cannot imagine it'.

However, the map also shows us the vulnerability to fire of much of our planet, especially in the context of increasing temperatures. Higher temperatures will draw more world regions, even in temperate zones, into the 'most exposed' category. Pausas notes that 'it's much easier to increase fire in a wet ecoregion

A band of fire swathes the Tropics. Map showing active fires during March 2010.

0.1

1.0

10

100

Fire pixels / 1000km² / day

with lush vegetation than in a dry region'. He goes on to explain that 'the sensitivity of fire to high temperatures is much stronger in high-productivity areas', implying that 'small changes in temperature have a much higher effect on fire activity in high-productivity areas'.

To the expert eye, the map already reveals human interference. According to the theory that vegetation and heat provide the best ingredients for fire, there should be more fire activity in the south of the US than there is. Pausas suspects that fire suppression practices have started to skew the pattern, meaning that fewer fires are happening in regions where plant life is historically adapted to them. Conversely, more fires are happening in some tropical areas than nature would predict. This may be because of deforestation and the consequent spread of more grasses and woody plants, which burn more readily than tropical forests.

ASTEROID STRIKES

Day

Night

• Smallest dot: 1 billion joules

● Biggest dot: 1,000,000 billion joules

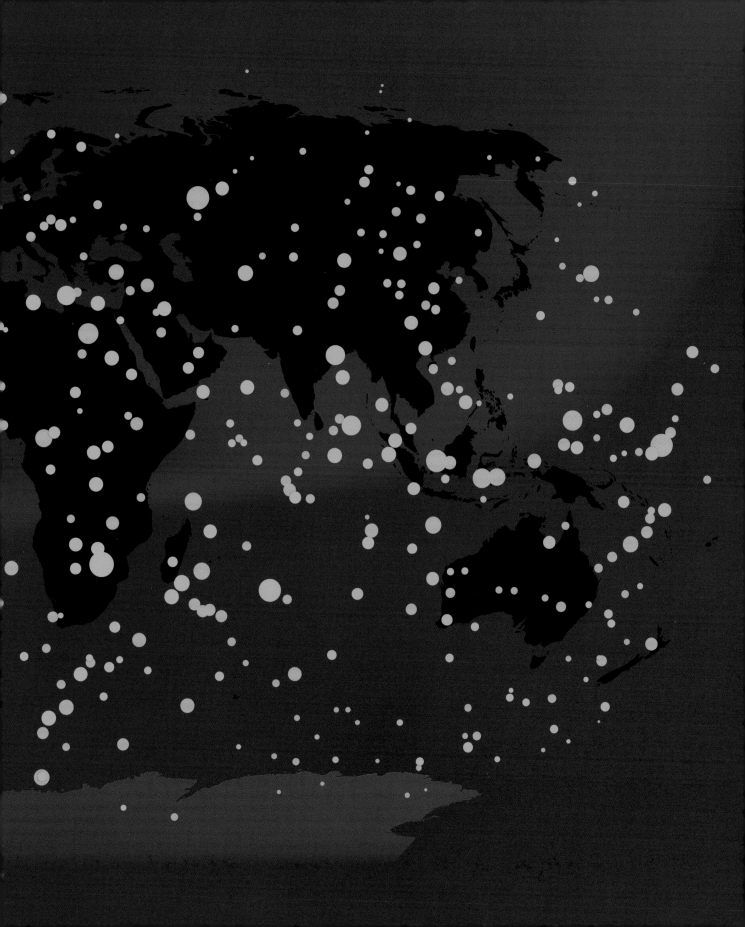

ASTEROID STRIKES

Our planet is bombarded by stuff from space. About a hundred tons of dust and sand-sized particles burn up in the atmosphere every day. The data this map is based on was released in November 2014 by NASA's Near-Earth Object Observations Program. It shows the global distribution of what are classed as small asteroid strikes, ranging in size from 3.5ft to 65.5ft (1m to 20m), over a twenty-year period from 1994 to 2013. The yellow dots are daytime strikes and the blue ones night-time strikes. The dots vary in size depending on the energy of the impact (measured in joules). They may be termed 'small' strikes, but the smallest dot on the map represents 1 billion joules of radiant energy, or about five tons of TNT explosives. The biggest dots represent up to 1 million billion joules, which is the equivalent of 1 million tons of TNT explosives.

The most obvious point the map makes is just how widespread strikes are. It shows a random pattern. No place is more likely to be hit, or not hit, than any other. This is not to say, however, that the chances of being hit at any one time are the same. Recent research suggests that there are certain times of year when the earth's orbit makes strikes more likely. North of the equator, November is the most likely month for getting hit by a meteorite, while May and June are the least likely. These are strikes on the earth's atmosphere. All asteroids break up in the atmosphere, making it down to the surface only in smaller fragments called meteorites. The largest strike on the map is represented by a yellow dot in Southern Russia. The large fireball seen over the skies of Chelyabinsk on the morning of 15 February 2013 was an asteroid of 56ft to 65.5ft (17m to 20m) in size, entering the earth's atmosphere at high speed. The resultant air blast damaged buildings across the city and caused hundreds of injuries, though, thankfully, no deaths.

The point of tracking all these impacts is to help us understand the scale and extent of the issue, and also to prepare us for even more significant and damaging strikes. The aim of the Near-Earth Object Observations Program is 'to find potentially hazardous asteroids before they find us,' explains project manager Donald Yeomans. About once a year, an asteroid the size of a car hits the earth's

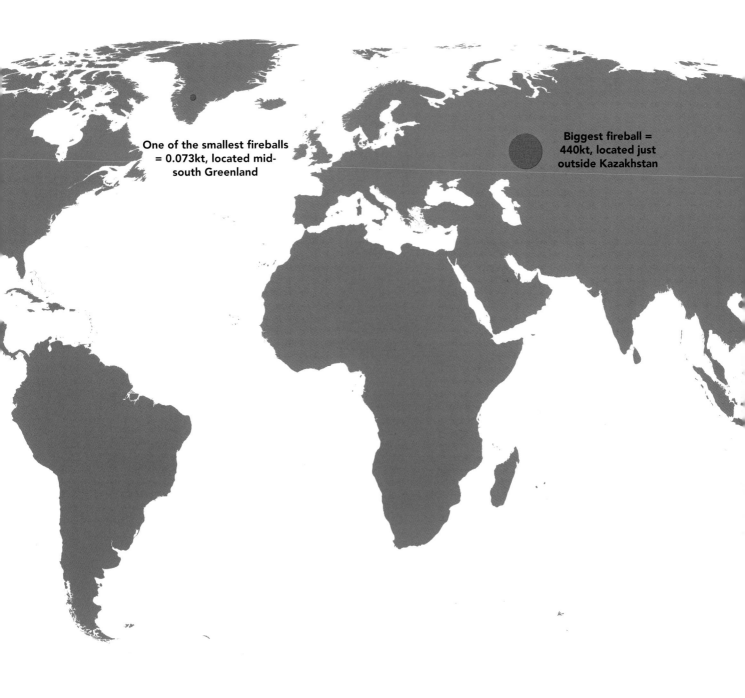

One of the smallest fireballs = 0.073kt, located mid-south Greenland

Biggest fireball = 440kt, located just outside Kazakhstan

kt = calculated total impact energy

Map showing the largest and one of the smallest asteroid strikes recorded between 15 April 1988 and 11 March 2017.

atmosphere, while once every five thousand years or so a football-field-sized asteroid strikes the atmosphere. Again on average, once every few million years there is a colossal impact, large enough to change radically and even extinguish life on earth.

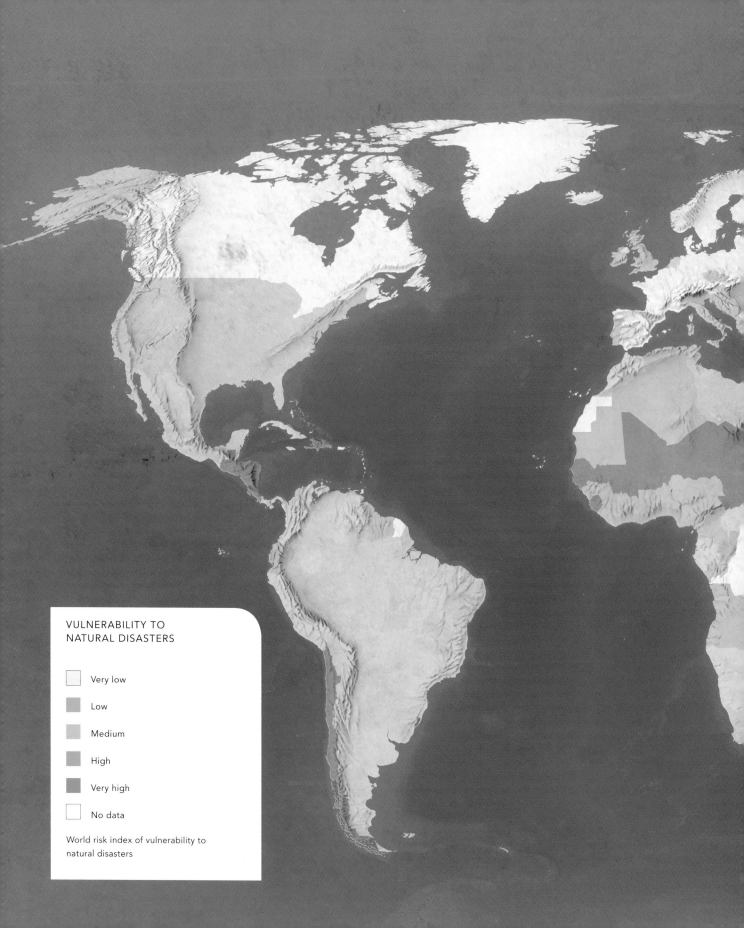

VULNERABILITY TO
NATURAL DISASTERS

◻ Very low

◻ Low

◻ Medium

◻ High

◻ Very high

◻ No data

World risk index of vulnerability to
natural disasters

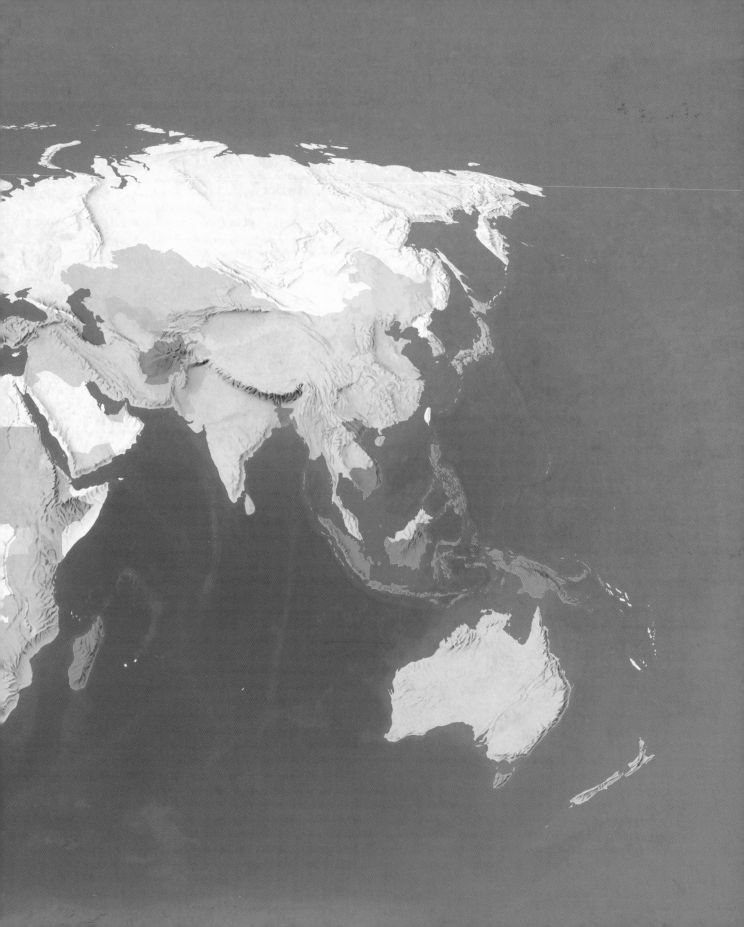

Earthquakes, droughts, floods and typhoons happen all the time. It is only when these events have catastrophic consequences for people that we pay attention to them. This map is based on the United Nations' 2012 *World Risk Report*, which identified the tiny Pacific island of Vanuatu as the most vulnerable spot on the planet, and Qatar, which is tucked away in a corner of the Arabian Peninsula, as the least.

Vanuatu suffers from being in an earthquake and cyclone zone without the resources to cope. It may be tiny, but the same thing can be said of the Philippines, its Pacific neighbour: with a population of 100 million, the Philippines is the third most vulnerable country. The map shows that the majority of the world's population lives in areas of medium to high risk. In most of these places, this reflects a lack of doctors, but also a lack of planning and a failure both to install and to maintain warning systems. The early-warning system put in place in many countries after a tsunami in the Indian Ocean in 2004 killed about 280,000, is a case in point. It worked well for three or four years, but it hasn't been maintained, with many early-warning buoys now lost or broken.

The academic who developed the risk index which the map is based on, Professor Jörn Birkmann of the University of Stuttgart, explains that 'the vulnerability of a country largely determines whether a natural hazard will turn into a disaster'. So if a typhoon hits the US, it will cause damage but is unlikely to be a disaster; if it hits the Philippines, many people will be in extreme danger. The bright green swathe of countries across Africa, indicating its acute vulnerability, drives the point home. The natural disaster most likely to affect this area is drought – a 'natural' disaster that adequate resources and preparation could remedy. This also explains why countries that sit side by side and face the same 'natural' risks can have very different levels of vulnerability. Haiti and Cuba, for example, or Yemen and Saudi Arabia: in each case there are the same risks, but with very different outcomes for each country.

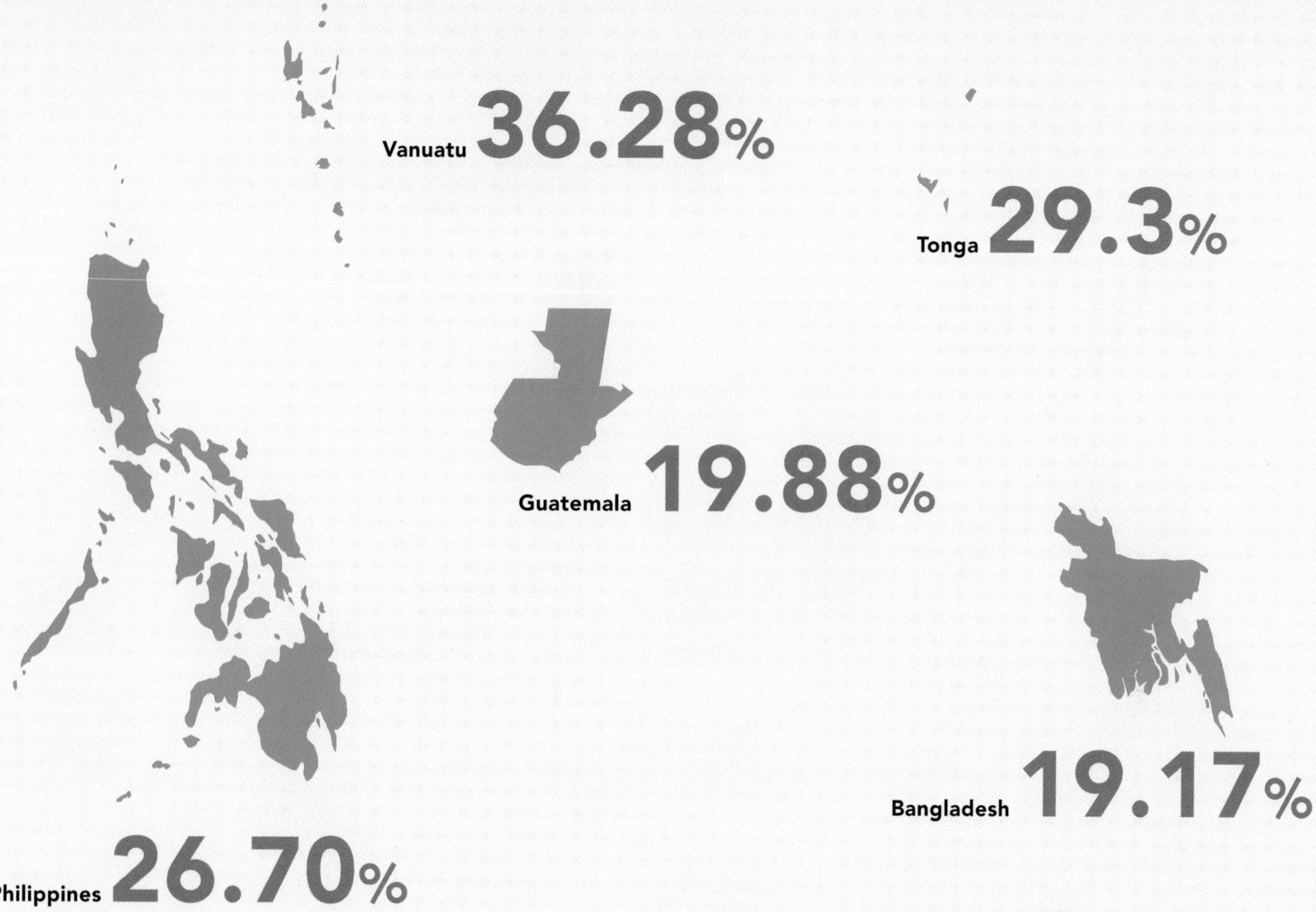

Vanuatu **36.28**%

Tonga **29.3**%

Guatemala **19.88**%

Bangladesh **19.17**%

Philippines **26.70**%

The top five countries most vulnerable to natural disasters in 2016. Their World Risk Index percentage is calculated by combining data on Coping, Exposure and Vulnerability.

Yet it would be a mistake to imagine that vulnerability can be made to disappear with more cash and education. Despite unrivalled preparation, Japan remains very vulnerable: there's only so much people can do to mitigate the impact of a major earthquake. There's no nation that can't be very quickly brought to its knees by Mother Nature. On average, natural disasters claim about 68,000 lives a year and severely impact a further 218 million (these figures are taken from the period between 1994 and 2013). An expanding population living in risky places, such as coastlines and megacities, as well as climate change and the depletion of natural defence systems (such as coastal sandbanks and swamps), means that most predictions point towards these figures going up rather than down.

It won't just be familiar catastrophes that drive up the figures. A new one to consider is the world's demographic arc, which spotlights an ageing and, therefore, more vulnerable population. Between 2010 and 2040 the number of people over 65 in less developed countries is expected to triple. Vulnerability is here to stay.

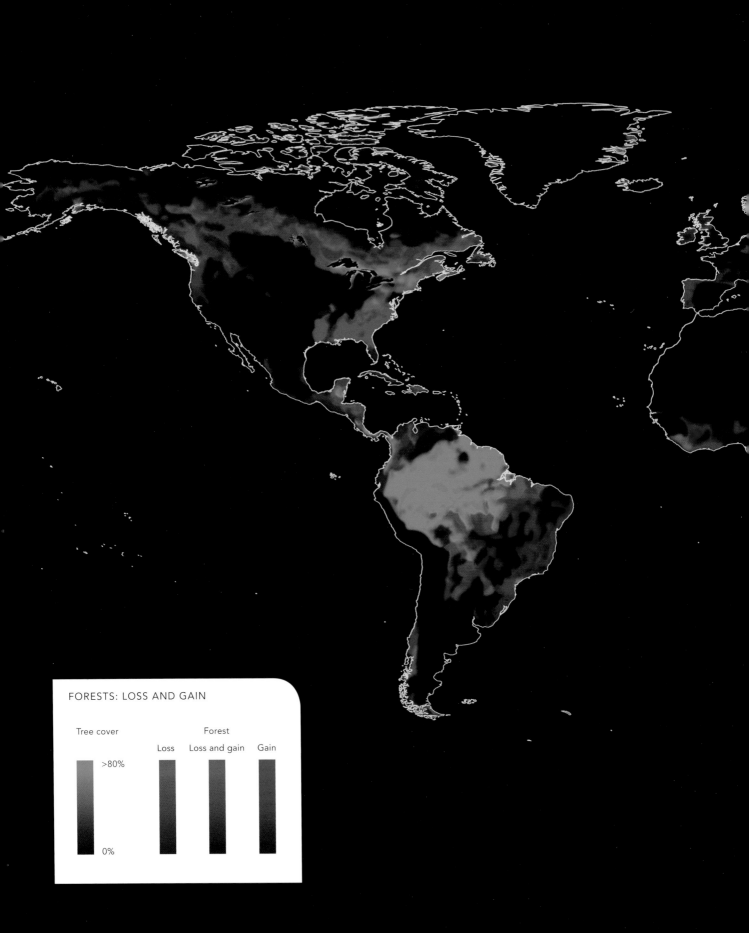

FORESTS: LOSS AND GAIN

Tree cover

>80%

0%

Forest

Loss   Loss and gain   Gain

The world is slowly waking up to the issue of forest loss. Unfortunately, this map shows that it's waking up only where it matters least. The red areas show loss, and the blue, gain. It's clear that there has been a reclamation of forest cover in some parts of North America, Europe and Russia, but in the Tropics, the most species-rich part of our planet, dramatic losses are ongoing. This remarkable image is based on satellite surveys made every year between 2000 and 2012. During that time, 888,000 square miles (almost 2,300,000km²) of forest were lost and 309,000 square miles (around 800,000km²) gained. Much of the gain was on land that had previously been forest before being cleared, and on abandoned agricultural land, notably in Russia.

The team of remote-sensing experts who created the original version of this map did an amazing job. The level of detail allows us to see how well particular conservation policies are working. Thus, although loss is clearly evident in Brazil, we can also see that the country's conservation measures are having an effect, for there is also forest gain. Some of the largest patches of loss in South America are in Bolivia, in the middle of the continent. Loss is also starkly evident in a number of countries in West and Central Africa.

The purple areas show both loss and gain, and usually indicate the presence of intensive forestry, with a continuous cycle of tree-felling and growth. Matthew Hansen, who led the remote-sensing team, explains: 'If you look at Finland and Sweden, it is patches of loss-gain, loss-gain, loss-gain across the whole country, which is just IKEA on the landscape – it is a forestry culture.' Something similar can be said about those areas of North America with intensive patterns of tree-planting and harvesting, notably in the south-east and north-west of the US and Canada.

Some have suggested that the map underplays the severity of forest loss. Since it is based on a definition of trees as 'all vegetation taller than 5m [16.5ft] in height', it includes monocultures of oil palm, rubber and Eucalyptus which have been planted on cleared forest land. Critics have claimed that 'classifying

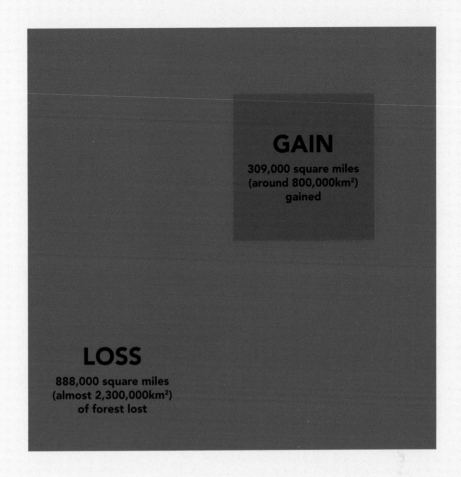

GAIN

309,000 square miles
(around 800,000km²)
gained

LOSS

888,000 square miles
(almost 2,300,000km²)
of forest lost

Forest lost and gained
between 2000 and 2012.

plantations as forests confuses an endangered habitat with its greatest threats'. Hansen and his team hit back by noting simply that they never claimed to be differentiating between the good and the bad. It's a fair point, and the map should be taken on its own terms. But the note of criticism usefully reminds us of the deep-seated assumptions so often brought to maps of the natural world. We assume that more forest, more growth is always a positive thing. It's a generalisation that is usually true but which, nevertheless, remains a generalisation.

WATER STRESS

Low stress <10–20%

Low to medium stress 10–20%

Medium to high stress 20–40%

High stress 40–80%

Extremely high stress >80%

No data

Ratio of withdrawals to supply

WATER STRESS

Water is our most precious resource; and an increasingly scarce one. 'Water stress' is a simple way of describing this situation. It is worked out by looking at the ratio between the use of water and its supply. High stress means that there is a small supply but high consumption. This snapshot is derived from 2013 data supplied by the World Resources Institute. The data was collected before large-scale famine and drought hit a large swathe of countries in West and East Africa. It shows an arc of high stress reaching all the way from Chile, up to Mexico and across to the countries bordering the Mediterranean, the entire Middle East and Central Asia and then down through India, Indonesia and finally arriving in Australia. It is a huge issue, and looks set to be one of the defining crises of the twenty-first century.

The list of countries with low water stress is pretty short. It includes a number of equatorial countries, such as Brazil, and several countries in Central Africa, where the presence of large rivers combines with a vast land area and small populations. However, this doesn't necessarily mean that people in those regions are getting decent water supplies. Many people in Sub-Saharan Africa still endure what is called 'economic water scarcity'. This is because they don't have a basic water service: they are without the pipe networks and other infrastructure that would allow them to benefit from what would otherwise be a plentiful water supply.

Water stress isn't about any and all water, but about fresh water – non-saline, drinkable water. The oceans hold around 97 per cent of the earth's water. We have plenty of water; what we don't have is much water that isn't salty. Fresh water is rare, and it is also very expensive to produce artificially.

There are some clever ways of joining these dots. In Hong Kong, about 80 per cent of residents flush their toilets with seawater, all thanks to a separate water distribution system set up in the 1950s. But it's not an idea that has taken off elsewhere. There are no easy solutions to water stress on offer.

Thirsty land. The countries in orange suffered the highest levels of water stress in 2013.

There are numerous reasons why water stress is a growing problem. The climate is changing, which means more rain for some people but less rain for most, especially in many of the grain-producing areas of the world. Then there is the expanding human population, much of it in areas already lacking sufficient water. The Middle East and North Africa are home to 6.3 per cent of the world's population but only 1.4 per cent of the world's renewable fresh water. It's no surprise that these areas are the most water-scarce regions of the world.

Most of the fresh water in these regions isn't drunk by people but is used in agriculture: irrigation is the big water consumer in the Middle East, as it is everywhere else. Agriculture accounts for over 90 per cent of fresh water use across the world. Water-intensive cereal grains such as wheat, rice and corn account for 27 per cent; meat production 22 per cent; and dairy 7 per cent. We need to switch to less water-hungry crops, and start planting drought-resistant grains such as millet and sorghum.

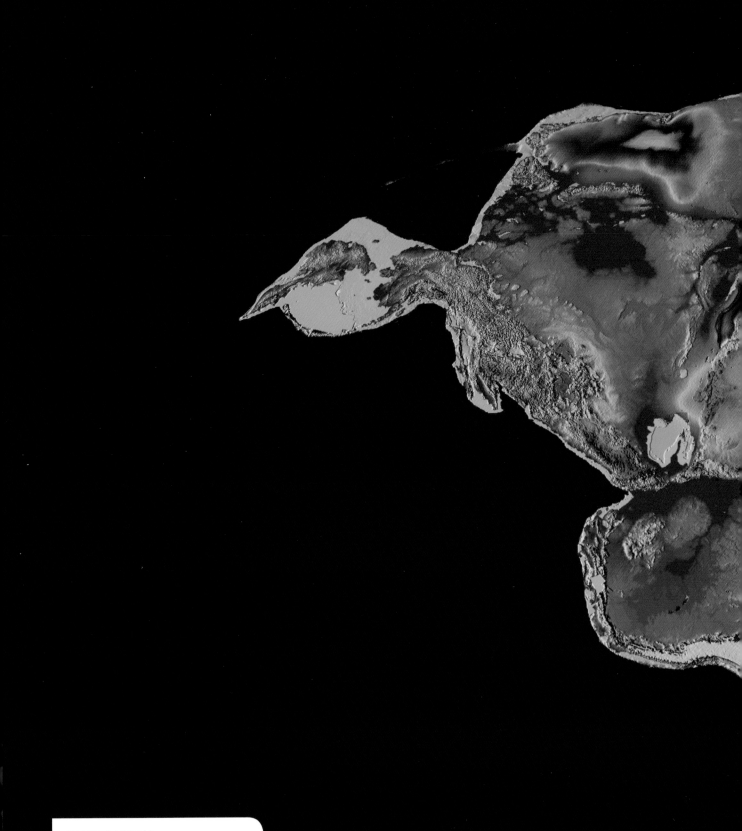

PANGEA ULTIMA

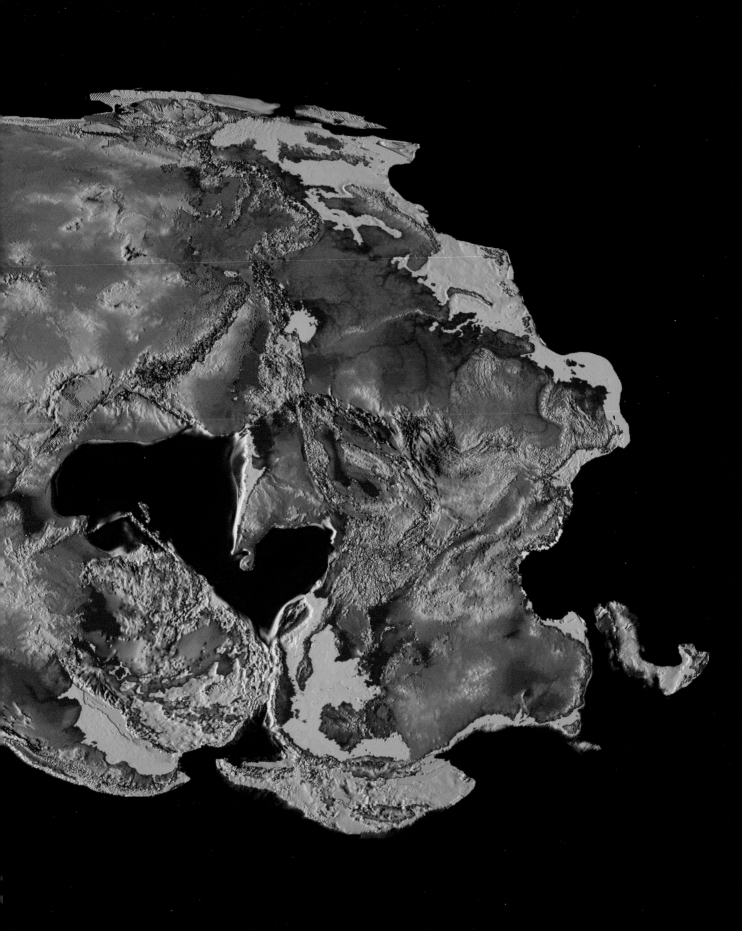

PANGEA ULTIMA

This isn't the world that was; it's the world that is to come. Pangea is the name that has been given to an ancient supercontinent, one that existed 300 million years ago. It broke up, and the continents we know today came into definition. But the movement of the great plates upon which the oceans and land sit hasn't come to an end. Based on our knowledge of past movements of these plates, we can roughly predict where we are headed, and it appears that that is straight back to where we came from. It's a place called Pangea Ultima.

In about 300 million years' time, our continents will have moved together again. If our very distant descendants are there to enjoy it, they will have the freedom to walk in a continuous trail from what was once Antarctica, up through Australia and Asia and down to the tip of South America, a journey that will afford many fine views over a vast inland ocean.

This speculative supercontinent is not the only possibility. Amasia and Novopangea are the names given to other contenders, but they all predict a return to a Pangea-like single mass. This amount of plate collision would produce considerable uplift, with new mountain chains being created in the areas where continents collide.

Models that leap less far into the future offer a more certain but similar scenario. The African plate, on which much of Southern Europe sits, has been colliding with Northern Europe for millions of years, creating the Alps and the Pyrenees. In about fifty million years, that process will have emptied the Mediterranean and pushed up a chain of mountains more akin to the mighty Himalayas than the modest Alpine peaks of today.

Despite these dramatic points of collision, it has to be said that Pangea Ultima does rather look like a badly made jigsaw of recognisable bits of the planet. This isn't a mistake, or cartographical laziness. Continents float on the earth's mantle (the layer just beneath the earth's crust), and it is down there where all the real geological action is. If they are not being directly pushed up or pulled down by the

An uncanny echo of the future from the past. The Anglo-Saxon Mappa Mundi (1025–1050) shows an early depiction of the world when it was believed to be one land mass. The East is shown at the top and the British Isles is located in the bottom left corner.

plates beneath them, continental shapes and even features like mountains suffer only slow erosion and persist for a long time.

Pangea Ultima is a geoprediction created by Dr Christopher Scotese, a geologist at the University of Texas. Talking about its strange shape, he muses that 'it's more like a big donut or bagel than Pangea', and admits that when naming it, 'I tried Bagelea or Donutea but figured that would trivialise the whole experience'. He settled on Pangea Ultima because it was 'classy, like a fancy car', but he is the first to acknowledge that the name's implication – that it's the end of a process, the last Pangea – 'certainly isn't true', adding, 'but it's the last one I'm going to come up with'.

Beyond Pangea Ultima there will be a continuous cycle of the breaking-apart of supercontinents, then the combination and collision of their parts into new Pangeas: the back-and-forth, squeeze-and-relax of a dynamic – perhaps the right word is 'living' – planet.

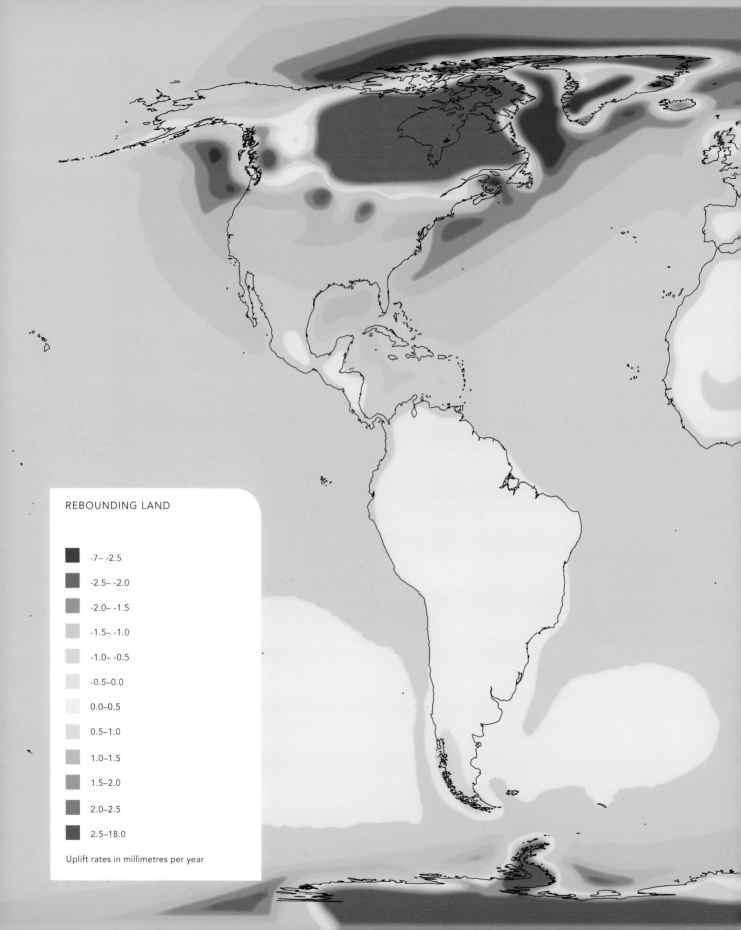

REBOUNDING LAND

- -7– -2.5
- -2.5– -2.0
- -2.0– -1.5
- -1.5– -1.0
- -1.0– -0.5
- -0.5–0.0
- 0.0–0.5
- 0.5–1.0
- 1.0–1.5
- 1.5–2.0
- 2.0–2.5
- 2.5–18.0

Uplift rates in millimetres per year

REBOUNDING LAND

The dark red and orange colours on this map indicate the earth's crust rebounding. It is a momentous process, for as some parts of the world rise up, others are sinking. Around 20,000 years ago great ice sheets, up to nearly 2 miles (3km) thick in places, covered much of Northern Europe, North America and Antarctica. The weight of all that ice pushed the earth's crust down by up to 1,640ft (0.5km). At the same time, land just beyond the ice sheets bulged upward by well over 1,000ft. Now that most of this ice is gone, the earth is readjusting itself.

The index on the map shows uplift – rebound – rates in millimetres per year. The scale takes us from a maximum of 0.7in (18mm) in the reddest patches to minus 0.02in (-7mm) in the darkest blue areas. These numbers may not sound very big and it is, in human terms, a slow process, but in geological terms this is dramatic stuff (though we should note that the average in the red areas is far less than 0.7in). The impacts of rebound are already clear. The fact that there are places far inland in Scandinavia called 'island' or 'skerry' gives us a clue. These patches used to be surrounded by water, but the whole landscape has risen up, and now they form small hills surrounded by forest and farmland.

For the same reason the Gulf of Bothnia, between Sweden and Finland, is slowly closing up. Indeed, the rate of rise there is so fast that one patch of it, around the Kvarken Archipelago, has been classed as a World Heritage Site by UNESCO because of its 'outstanding geological and geomorphological attributes'. UNESCO explains that as it lifts 'at rates that are among the highest in the world', so 'islands appear and unite, peninsulas expand, lakes evolve from bays and develop into marshes and peat fens'. The downside of this uplift is felt further south in Europe.

Some nations pivot on the issue, such as the UK, where once-ice-covered Scotland and the north of England are rebounding and the south is sliding downward. As the maps suggests, the biggest areas of ice were centred over Canada and Greenland. Now these parts are rising up and, as a consequence, much of the US is sinking. But it is not just a simple North–South see-saw. The map also shows that there are areas just around the fast-rising zones that have

The shape of the Earth is deformed by many forces. This model from 2011 shows the shape that the surface of the oceans would take under the influence of Earth's gravity and rotation alone. Red indicates high levels of gravity and blue, low levels.

the greatest rates of fall. These adjacent zones are what glacial geologists call the 'fore bulges', the areas just next to the ice sheet that were once tilted up and which are now undergoing the most extreme descent.

The forces of mountain creation, of uplift and subduction, seen at the interface of tectonic plates, are not shown on this map, which restricts itself to ice rebound. There is nothing humans can do about any of these mighty geological events. They are important to understand, though, as they can exacerbate the problems of rising sea levels in areas such as Western and Central Europe and the US.

Where rebound is happening, it is making a real difference, even to the point of causing new arguments about land ownership. In rebounding areas, to whom does the new land, now raised from the sea, belong? The answer is usually that it belongs to the person who owned the water, not the shore. But it is less clear how this works for land that is slipping into the sea; or, indeed, if nations with retreating coastlines should either start building new artificial islands or begin pegging back their territorial waters.

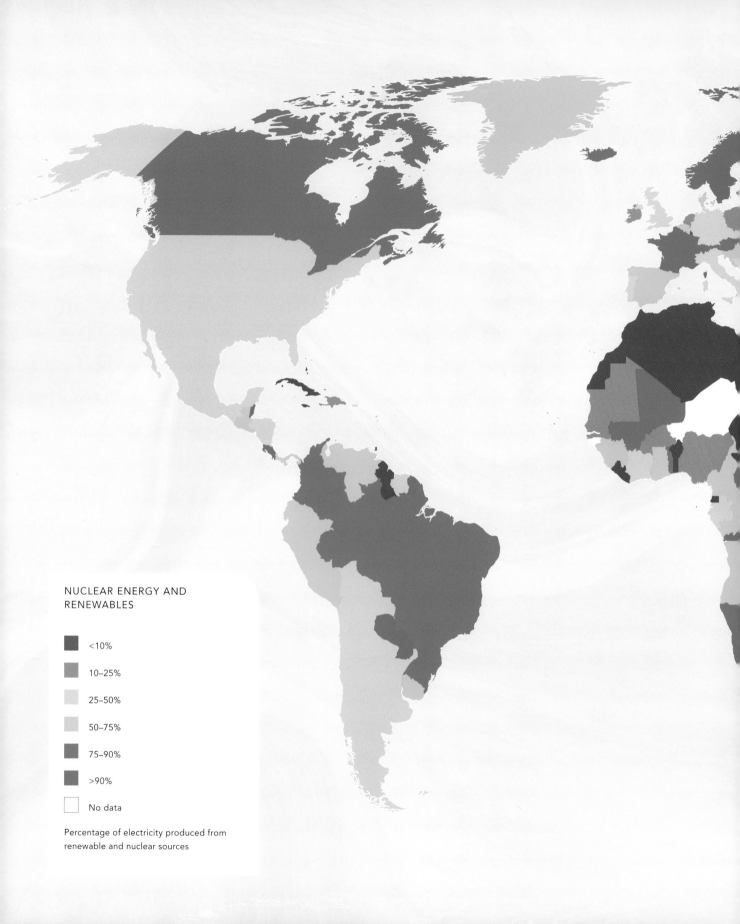

NUCLEAR ENERGY AND
RENEWABLES

- <10%
- 10–25%
- 25–50%
- 50–75%
- 75–90%
- >90%
- No data

Percentage of electricity produced from
renewable and nuclear sources

NUCLEAR ENERGY AND RENEWABLES

There is no shortage of energy in the world, but there is a shortage of efficient ways to access it. Some nations are doing a lot better than others, and this map has some surprises about which ones. We know that Norway, Sweden and Finland derive a lot of their electricity from water power, but what are those larges patches of dark green in Africa and in South America? It turns out that when it comes to renewables, it is this often overlooked but tried and tested resource – hydropower – that has enabled nations both rich and poor to turn away from hydrocarbons.

Hydropower is by far and away the biggest source of renewable energy. About 95 per cent of renewable energy in the US is hydroelectric power. Hydropower makes up nearly 100 per cent of electricity production in Paraguay; so rich in water power is this landlocked South American country that it has become one of its biggest exports – Paraguay sends 90 per cent of its generated energy to its neighbours. Ethiopia generates most of its electricity from dams on the Blue Nile, and in the Democratic Republic of Congo, more than 95 per cent of electricity comes from hydro, much of it from two big dams 140 miles (225km) to the south of the capital, Kinshasa. In fact, Congo could generate even more: it has been estimated that it has the potential to supply 13 per cent of the world's hydropower. It also has hundreds of solar power systems and vast biogas reserves.

It isn't hydro but nuclear energy that helps France come out so well on this map. Ukraine and Hungary also produce more than half of their electricity from nuclear plants. Perhaps the biggest surprise is how little renewable development there has been in many of the countries with the greatest potential for solar power. North Africa and the Middle East are still reliant on oil, and the South African government has failed to commission significant renewable energy programmes.

Renewables are a fast-changing resource, and this map doesn't capture some of the biggest developments that are in progress. China is investing heavily in solar power, and it is estimated that by 2020, over 15 per cent of the country's energy capacity will come from non-fossil fuel sources. There are ambitious plans to turn solar power generated in the hot, cloudless skies of North Africa into the

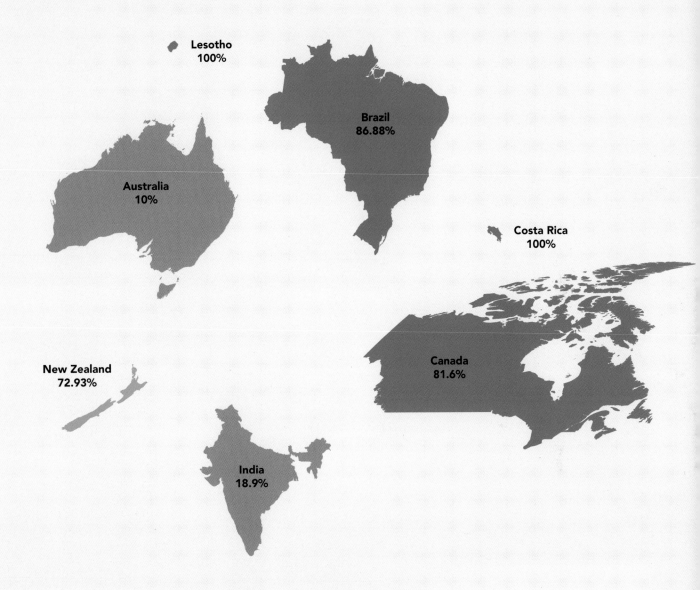

Lesotho
100%

Brazil
86.88%

Australia
10%

Costa Rica
100%

Canada
81.6%

New Zealand
72.93%

India
18.9%

Lesotho and Costa Rica generate all their electricity from renewable sources, unlike many, much richer countries like Australia.

energy base for Europe. The energy the sun pours down onto the earth's deserts in six hours is more than the world consumes in a year. 'Desert power' promises to slash the cost of energy bills as well as curb carbon emissions. Yet a lot of these schemes are just that – still at the 'on paper' stage. The world awaits the massive boom in solar energy, while hydropower is already up and running, transforming a number of countries that have huge rivers and lakes into centres of green energy.

AIR POLLUTION

Low

High

Carbon monoxide concentrations in spring
measured between 2000 and 2004

AIR POLLUTION

Carbon monoxide is a deadly gas that you can't smell or see. It is produced by incomplete combustion. One of its main causes is forest fires, but this map shows us that it is also an industrial and urban pollutant. That huge red blob is perverse proof that East Asia is the workshop of the world, but it also points the finger at the vast number of combustion engines chugging away down there.

This map shows average carbon monoxide concentrations in spring between 2000 and 2004. It is one of many global maps of different types of pollution which we can now access, thanks to specialised scientific instruments that have been installed on satellites. The Measurement of Pollution in the Troposphere (MOPITT) equipment that took this particular image sits on a NASA satellite and continuously scans the earth's atmosphere. MOPITT sweeps 400-mile-wide (644km-wide) bands of the earth every four days, giving us a global picture that is invaluable when we want to see where the problem areas are and whether anti-pollution initiatives are making any difference.

Before satellites started looking at pollution, we couldn't see the big picture. Researchers had to rely on extrapolating data from local studies. The tireless, enduring and ever-circling MOPITT deserves to be better known. Only a couple of decades ago we understood little about the global distribution of toxins such as carbon monoxide, but now there's no excuse for ignorance.

Carbon monoxide is a poisonous gas whose concentrations show significant geographic variability and seasonality. You can only really get the complete and complex picture by looking at a whole series of images. It would be a mistake to look at this particular map and conclude that South America and Africa are untroubled by high carbon monoxide levels – wherever there is combustion you will find carbon monoxide. Although the red mists over East Asia are a chronic and disturbing feature, other maps from MOPITT show sudden eruptions of carbon monoxide in Russia, Africa, South America and Australia, often as a result of forest fires or seasonal patterns of agricultural burning.

2000
130 ppbv

2007
115 ppbv

Carbon monoxide

2014
105 ppbv

Carbon monoxide levels have decreased by almost twenty per cent between 2000 and 2014. Measured in parts per billion by volume (ppbv).

MOPITT brings good news as well as bad. Overall concentrations of carbon monoxide have declined since 2000, especially in the northern hemisphere, where greener cars and cleaner industries are making a real and tangible difference to people's lives. There have even been slight decreases of carbon monoxide over China, although similar instruments on board roving satellites have shown that other pollutants are on the rise. The NASA satellite and maps such as these enable us to monitor the situation, and to use our observations to make a difference.

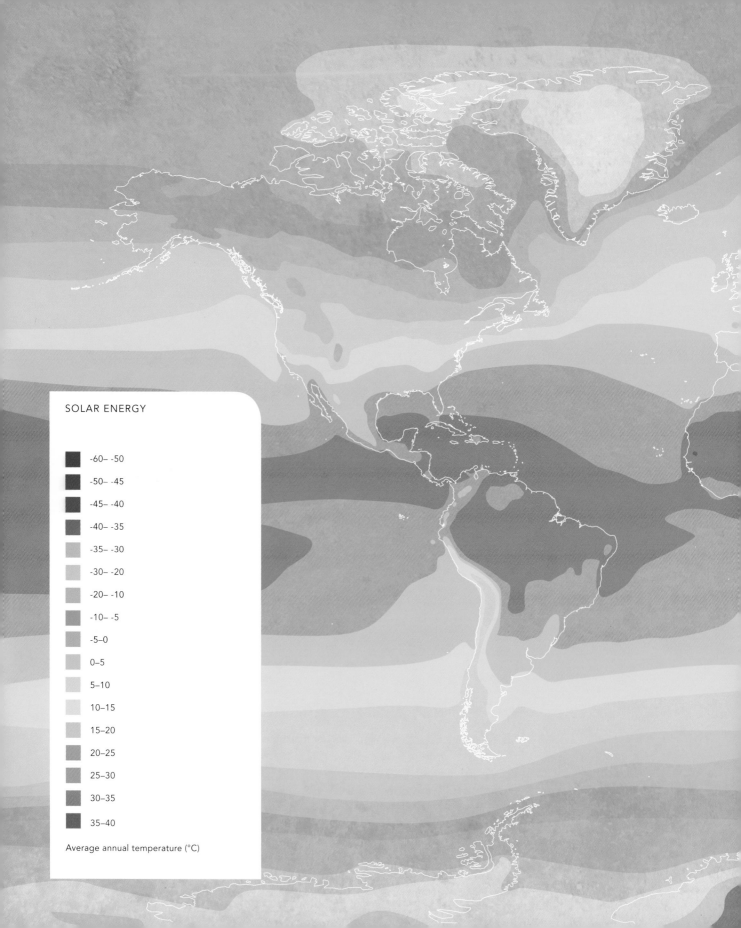

SOLAR ENERGY

▪	-60– -50
▪	-50– -45
▪	-45– -40
▪	-40– -35
▪	-35– -30
▪	-30– -20
▪	-20– -10
▪	-10– -5
▪	-5–0
▪	0–5
▪	5–10
▪	10–15
▪	15–20
▪	20–25
▪	25–30
▪	30–35
▪	35–40

Average annual temperature (°C)

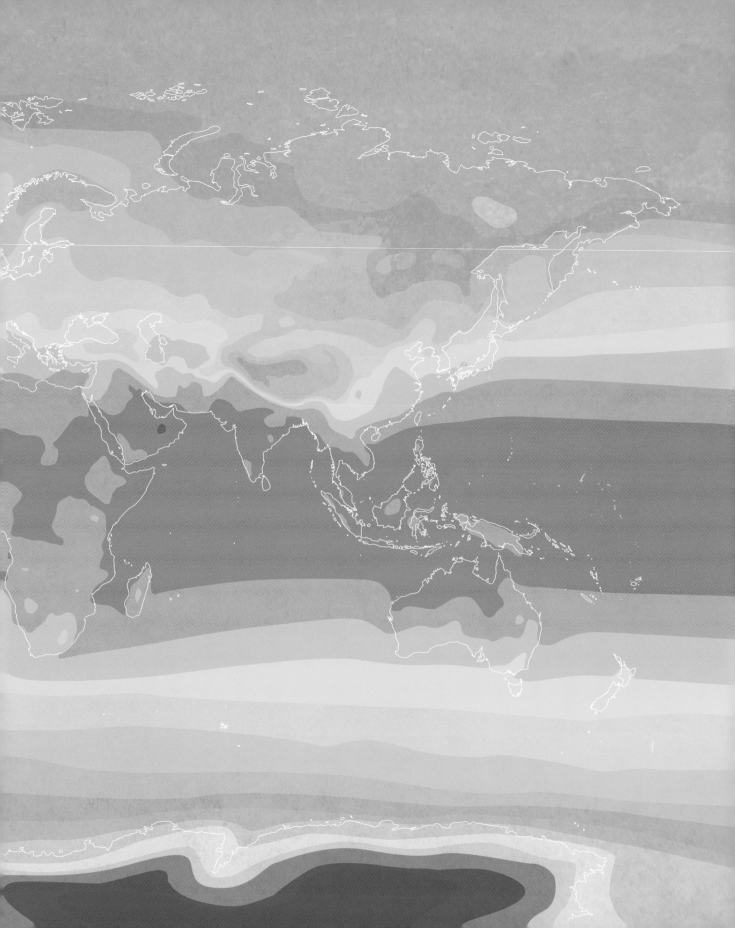

SOLAR ENERGY

Every year the sun transmits enough solar power to earth to supply more than 1,000 times our current energy needs. This map shows us average yearly surface temperatures across the planet. It illustrates how much of that energy is pouring down onto the seas as well as the land. There is a thick band of heat across the Indian and Pacific Oceans, a band which breaks up over Africa, South America and the Atlantic. It is also noticeable just how much colder the Antarctic is than the Arctic.

One of the factors that affect temperature is height above sea level. For instance, despite being on the same latitude as the Sahara, the Himalayas and the Tibetan Plateau, just north of India, remain cold. Mountains and hills also help explain some of the variability in temperature we see on the continents of Africa and South America.

The influence of ocean currents that either pour warm water into cooler latitudes or cold water into tropical seas can also be seen to be at work. The British Isles are more temperate than their high position in the northern hemisphere would suggest they should be, because of a warm current sweeping up through the North Atlantic. Conversely, the western seaboards of Africa and South America are chilled by a cold current that flows up from the southern seas.

Another factor that has a cooling or warming effect is the prevailing wind. For example, the wind tends to blow from a south-westerly direction over Northwestern Europe, helping to create that bulge of yellow seen on the map over that part of the world. Based on a yearly average, our map doesn't show the great differences in temperature that can exist between regions in the same colour zone. Places in the middle of a continent can have extremely hot summer temperatures and very cold winter temperatures, while countries next to the sea, such as the UK, are mild all year round.

Given the crises over climate change and energy supply, it is not surprising that maps like this have been seized upon as evidence of the urgent need to start harvesting solar power. It has been claimed that the entire world's power

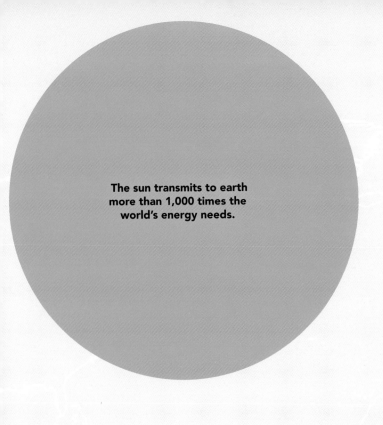

The sun transmits to earth more than 1,000 times the world's energy needs.

1.5

Just 1.5 per cent of the Sahara can feed the world's energy needs through solar power.

needs could be supplied from the solar energy that falls in just 1.5 per cent of the Sahara. Given that only around 30 per cent of Sub-Saharan Africans have access to electricity, both the need and the potential are vast. The first phase of the world's largest solar power plant opened in 2016 in Southern Morocco, and will be generating enough electricity to power a million homes by 2018. All that power gifted by the sun falling onto the world's emptiest and most barren regions is finally being put to work.

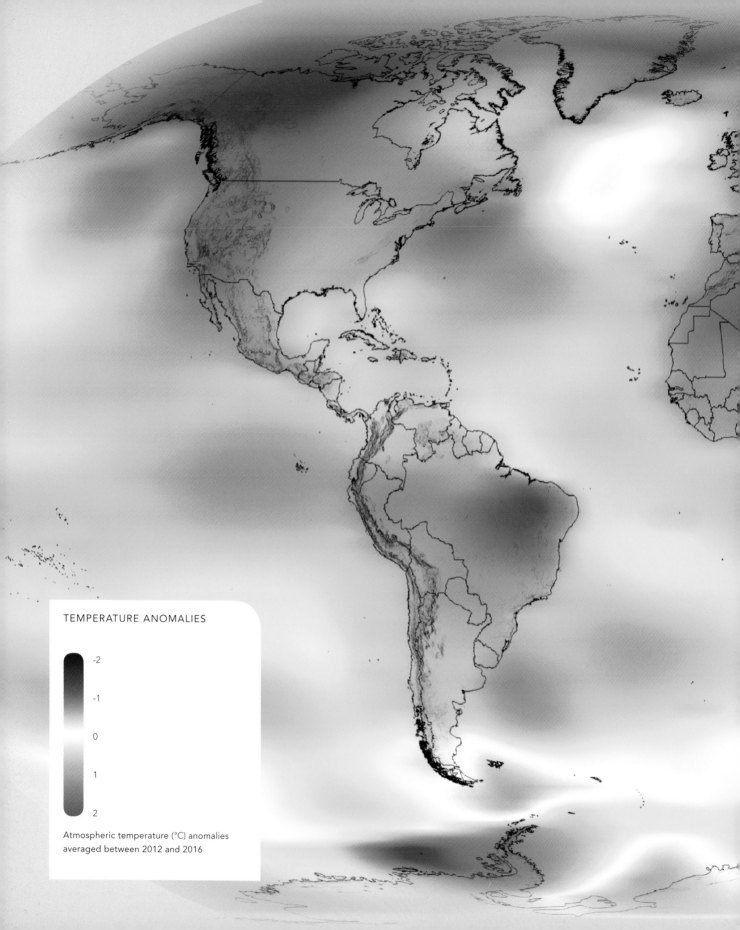

TEMPERATURE ANOMALIES

-2
-1
0
1
2

Atmospheric temperature (°C) anomalies
averaged between 2012 and 2016

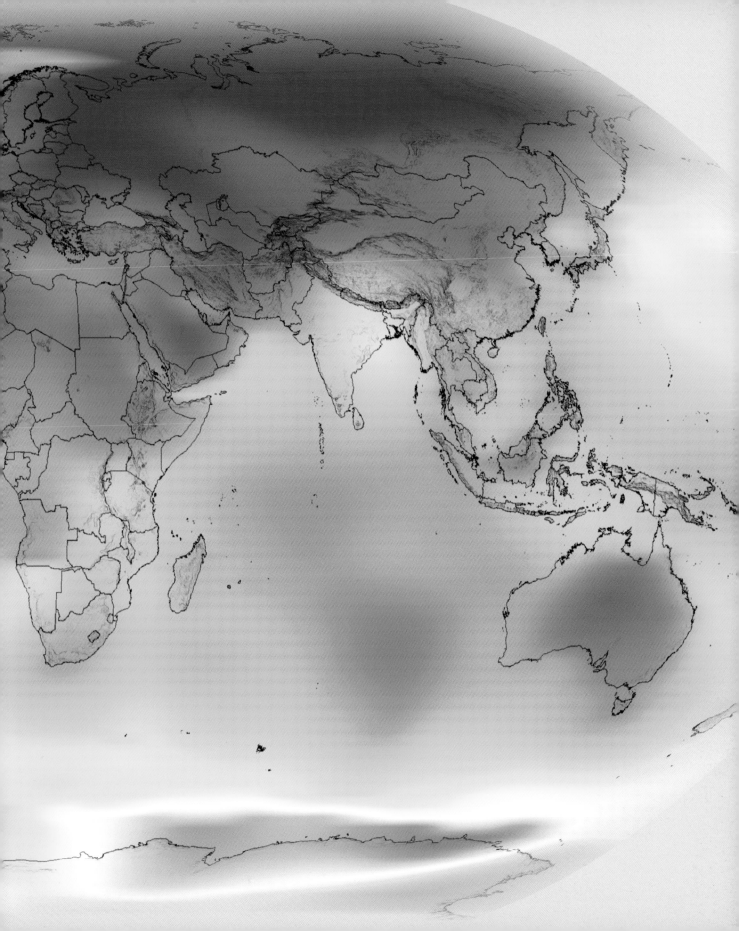

According to Gavin Schmidt, director of NASA's Goddard Institute for Space Studies, '2016 is remarkably the third record year in a row . . . We don't expect record years every year, but the ongoing long-term warming trend is clear.' The average temperature in 2016 was 0.99°C (1.78°F) higher than it was in the mid-twentieth century. That doesn't sound like a lot, but the rise is beginning to look consistent and continual. Since 1880, when records began, sixteen of the seventeen warmest years on record have occurred since 2001. Worldwide temperatures in July 2016 were the hottest for any month since 1880. The last year that was cooler than average was 1976.

This map shows us changes in the earth's surface temperature averaged between 2012 and 2016. Orange colours represent temperatures that are warmer and blues represent temperatures that are cooler than a baseline period between 1951 and 1980.

The swirling and pulsing shades of orange picture an uneven process. The darkest, almost red, areas in the far north contrast with the patches of blue in the southern oceans. 2016 was the warmest year ever in the Arctic, leading to a record low of sea ice. Darker shades can also be seen sweeping down through much of Europe and into the Middle East, as well as centring on Brazil and much of Australia. Many of these places are already hot, so all that extra heat has particularly severe consequences. For example, Australia is, on average, 8°C (46.40°F) hotter than the rest of the world; widespread drought and livestock death are just two problems facing Australia as it gets even hotter, problems that are not faced by countries such as the UK, which are warming from a much cooler baseline.

These local trends are, for the most part, just darker hues of orange against a background of orange: hotspots in a hot world. One of the questions the map throws up is why Antarctica and its surrounding seas are not warming up. In fact, they are cooling. One theory is that the ocean currents and high winds around the southern continent may be helping to isolate it from a warming world. Since the

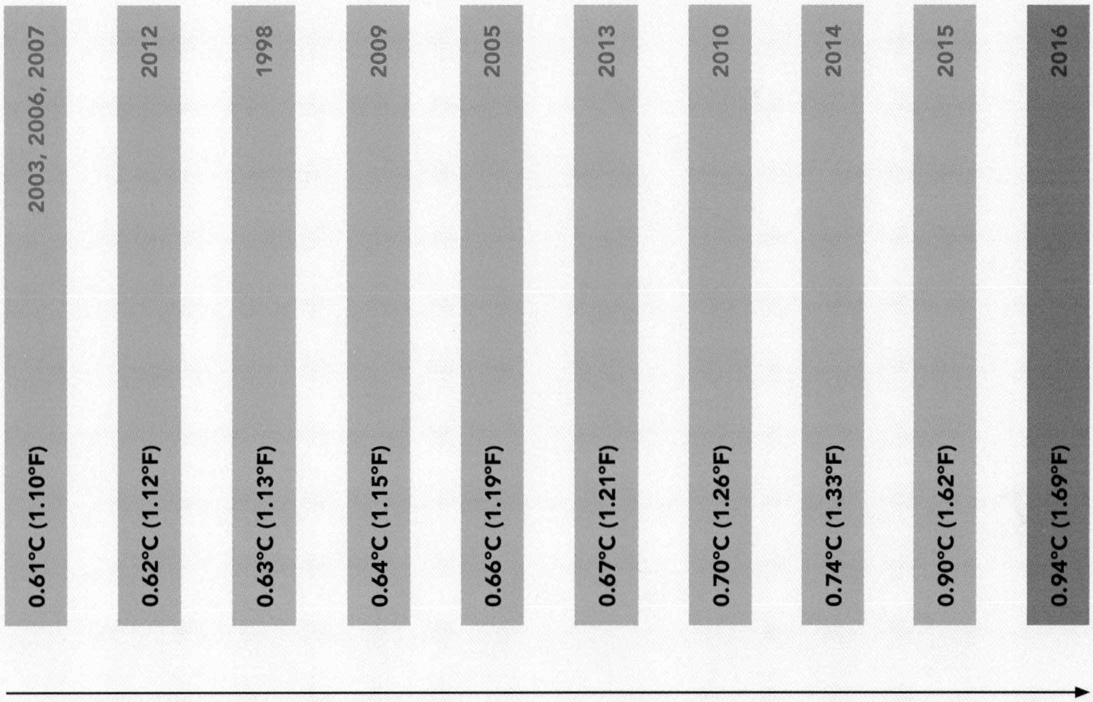

2003, 2006, 2007 — 0.61°C (1.10°F)

2012 — 0.62°C (1.12°F)

1998 — 0.63°C (1.13°F)

2009 — 0.64°C (1.15°F)

2005 — 0.66°C (1.19°F)

2013 — 0.67°C (1.21°F)

2010 — 0.70°C (1.26°F)

2014 — 0.74°C (1.33°F)

2015 — 0.90°C (1.62°F)

2016 — 0.94°C (1.69°F)

Warmest years since 1880 when records began, with anomalies relative to the twentieth century average.

late 1970s, while the Arctic has lost an average of 20,800 square miles (53,872km^2) of sea ice per year, the Antarctic has gained an annual average of 7,300 square miles (18,907km^2). We have long thought of the Arctic and Antarctic as twins, as mirrors of each other, but increasingly this isn't true; they appear to have very different destinies.

The data that this map is based on was collected by NASA from a vast network of meteorological instruments across the world. These include 6,300 weather stations, ship- and buoy-based observations of the surface temperature of the sea as well as measurements made at Antarctic research stations. Data is then analysed and corrected for anything that might distort the figures, such as the heat created by neighbouring cities.

AIR TRAFFIC

◯ Size = number of flights

◐ Colour = longitude

3,200 airports
60,000 routes

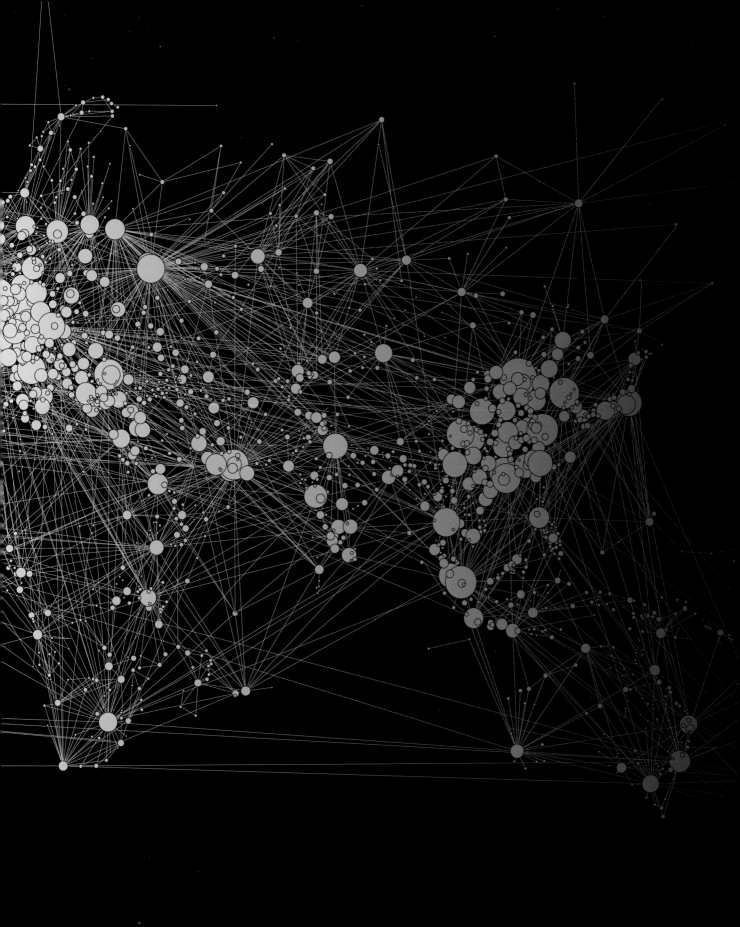

AIR TRAFFIC

Here is a world woven over with lines of flight. They knot themselves in dense, bright tangles in some places, only to be teased out into yawning black holes in others. Irrespective of recession, taxes and terrorism, the number of flights keeps on growing. Global passenger numbers were up over six per cent in 2016, and have been rising at about or above that rate for years. Industry forecasters confidently predict growth all the way to 2030. The weave will get tighter and evermore brilliant. And the gaps in the fabric will start filling up.

In fact, what is striking about this map is just how many empty zones there still are. Africa has barely two per cent of the world's air traffic (equated with revenue-paying passengers multiplied by distance travelled). At thirty-one per cent, Asia has more than Europe, but as it is a continent that is so vast and populous, that's a low figure. Certainly its skies aren't laced with contrails like those of Northwestern Europe. So what at first glance looks like a very contemporary vision of the world turns out to be oddly backward-looking. The rise of the Asian economies and the shift of world industry to the East has not yet been mirrored in air traffic terms.

Even the Gulf States, where airport-building has been frenzied, still don't have anything like the heft of air travel that we see in Europe. Despite the fact that Qatar has one of the highest numbers of passenger arrivals per million of its population (618,362 seats per million people), this map shows us a planet where the North Atlantic is the dominant airline hub: a world where Europe and the US hold centre stage.

So what's going on? Air traffic is an expensive way of transporting goods, the majority of which go by sea. And the swelling middle classes of China and India, nations with a billion-plus people each, have yet to gain access to mass air travel. This is about to change. Here is a map on the brink of becoming a historical curiosity. The big growth in air traffic is coming from those holes in the weave: from Asia, Latin America and the fast-growing economies of Africa.

A much denser web of flights is being pulled across the planet, connecting peoples as well as opening up societies and making them more alike. It is not just

Qatar

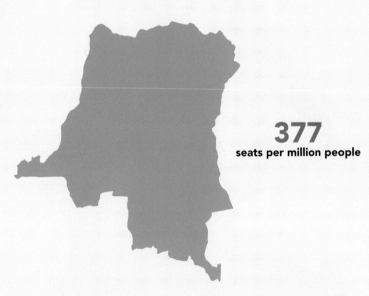

618,362
seats per million people

Democratic Republic of Congo

377
seats per million people

Qatar has the largest ratio of seats per million people with over 1,600 times more seats than the Democratic Republic of Congo.

a technological or an economic change; it's also a psychological, even a moral shift. Ask people today what they have been up to and they will tell you where they have been. Remaining in one place is a kind of modern sin, a reflection of inertia and failure. In this new vision of the world, to be is to go.

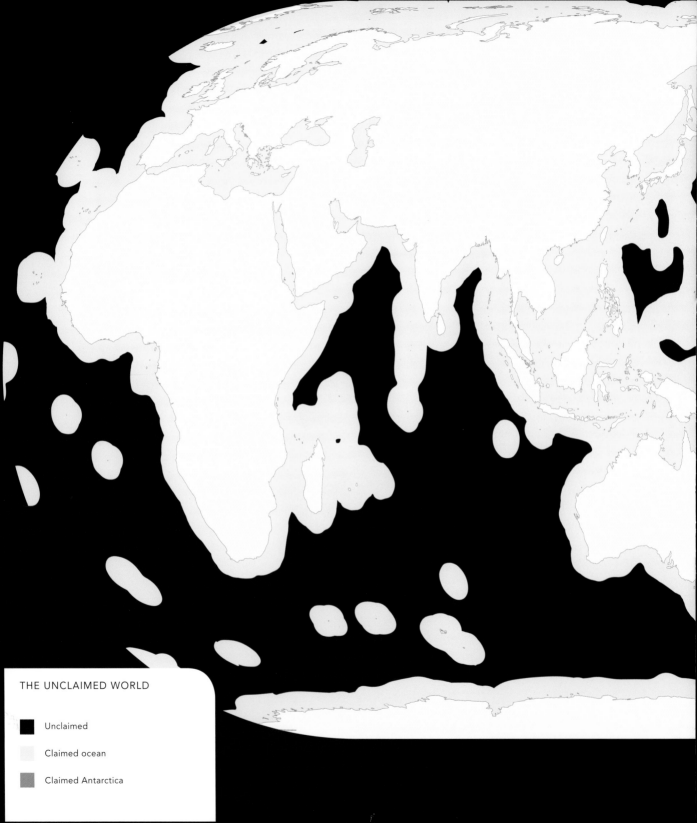

THE UNCLAIMED WORLD

■ Unclaimed

Claimed ocean

Claimed Antarctica

THE UNCLAIMED WORLD

It is useful to be reminded that most of the world's surface is not part of any nation. The unclaimed planet is a watery thing, though there remains a large cut of Antarctica which also lies untaken. The rest of that continent was split up by the Antarctic Treaty of 1959, ratified between seven nations (Argentina, Australia, Chile, France, New Zealand, Norway and the United Kingdom).

The unclaimed world usually starts 200 nautical miles (370km) out from the average low waterline on a country's shore. Before this lies the 'exclusive economic zone', which, unlike 'territorial waters' (extending to just 12 nautical miles (22km) from shore), isn't owned by anyone but which, nevertheless, is only available to be exploited by that particular nation. Given the oil, gas and many other resources that exist beneath the seabed – resources which have been depleted on land – this exclusive zone is a very valuable asset. Nations with long shorelines have an inbuilt economic advantage. That's especially true for small countries such as Denmark, which has exclusive access to the vast zones around its distant, autonomous territory of Greenland.

One way to extend this zone is by building islands on the high seas, a measure currently being pursued by China which, so far, has met with little resistance. It's the kind of activity that suggests it is not far-fetched to imagine that one day the whole world will be incorporated into 'exclusive zones'.

The high seas are free, and any nation or, indeed, any person can fish, sail and do whatever else they want out there – in theory. The reality is a little more complicated. According to the United Nations Convention on the Law of the Sea, 'every State shall effectively exercise its jurisdiction and control in administrative, technical and social matters over ships flying its flag'. So even when you are in international waters your vessel is, legally, a little bit of the country where it is registered. In fact, some countries push this claim even further. The US claims 'Special Maritime and Territorial Jurisdiction' over 'any place outside the jurisdiction of any nation with respect to an offense by or against a national of the United

71

71% of the earth is covered by ocean

45

The high seas cover 45% of the earth's surface

64

64% of the ocean is considered the high seas / international water

States'. International law also recognises the right of countries to act against grave offences in international waters such as piracy, human trafficking or terrorism.

Thus this is not a map of places entirely without law, or where the state can never reach you. Another caveat: the term 'unclaimed' should, perhaps, be preceded by 'internationally recognised'. One of the more confusing chapters of the United Nations Convention on the Law of the Sea is where it recognises a nation's claim on its continental shelf, a geological concept that has become mired in geopolitics. A continental shelf can stretch out for up to 400 miles (644km) into the sea, but defining where and why it begins and ends has proved contentious.

So it isn't quite true to say that the blue on the map is not claimed by anyone, just that those claims don't yet have international approval. Many of these 'unrecognised' claims concern the Arctic. Canada claimed the North Pole in 1925, and since then there have been a raft of other would-be owners. The Russian Arktika 2007 expedition dived to the seabed directly below the pole and planted a Russian flag. They want it, but is it theirs? The unclaimed world is increasingly a realm of claims and counterclaims.

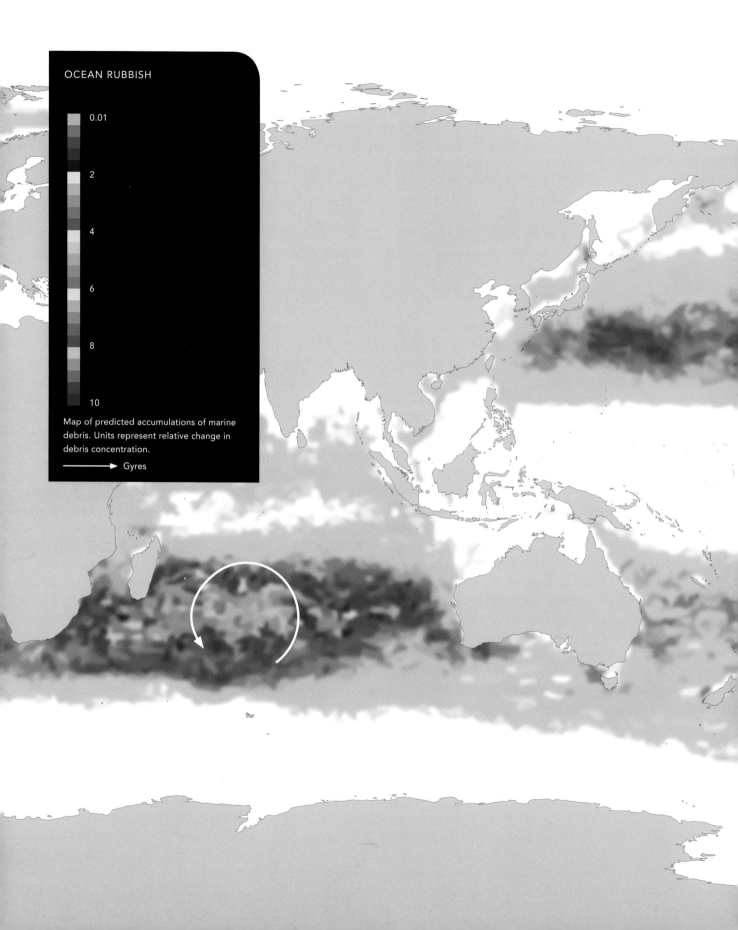

OCEAN RUBBISH

0.01

2

4

6

8

10

Map of predicted accumulations of marine
debris. Units represent relative change in
debris concentration.

→ Gyres

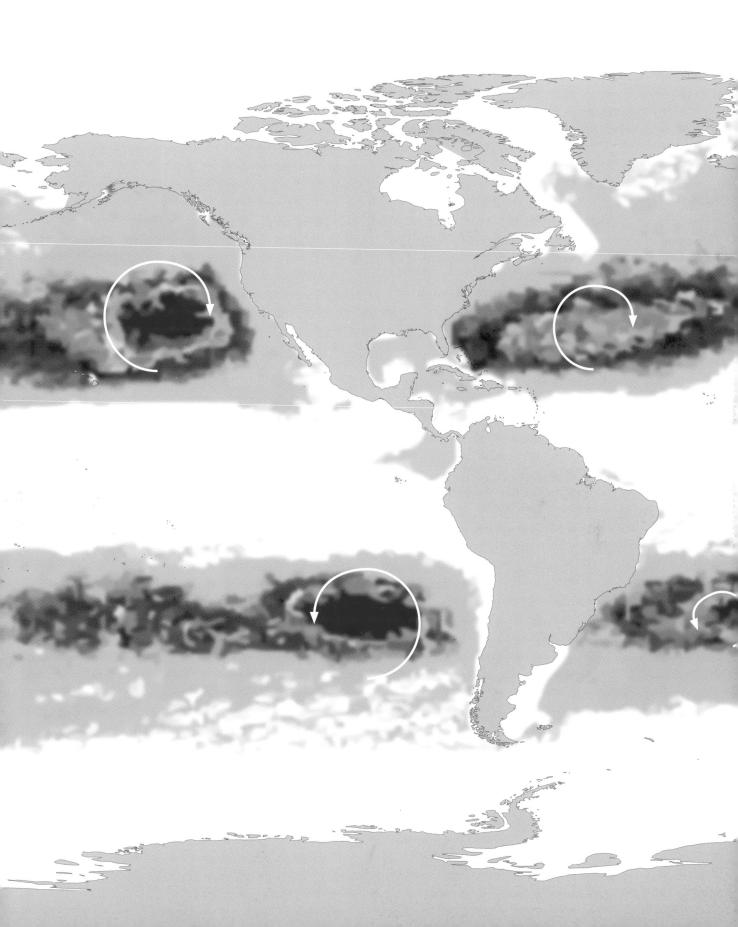

OCEAN RUBBISH

Estimates of the size of the Pacific Trash Vortex range between 270,000 square miles (almost 700,000km^2) and 5,800,000 square miles (around 15,000,000km^2). Also known as the Great Pacific Garbage Patch, it does not exist as a single entity but is more like a soup or galaxy of rubbish, most of which floats just below the water but which often gloops together on the surface.

All the things that are thrown off ships or swept up off the coasts of the Pacific Ocean, getting caught in its circulation, end up in this graveyard of consumerism. About 20 per cent of ocean plastic comes from ships, while the rest washes out to sea from beaches or is carried downstream in rivers. Footballs, kayaks and LEGO blocks have all been spotted, along with the usual mass of plastic bottles and fishing net. The combination of ocean currents and floating, very durable rubbish, is creating a growing mess.

Plastic is amazing stuff: it is one of the lightest, most useful yet most hard-wearing of materials, and we make around 295,500 tons (300,000 tonnes) of it every year. It takes between 500 and 1,000 years for plastic to degrade. Every decade, production of plastic more than doubles. Most of it is not being recycled, and has therefore now become a major source of marine pollution. It chokes the life out of the oceans. It has been estimated that in the centre of the Great Pacific Garbage Patch, almost half a square mile (1.3km^2) contains 480,000 pieces of plastic. Because animals are eating fragments of this debris, they are taking in toxic pollutants. A recent study of fish collected from the Pacific found that over one third had ingested plastic particles.

The map is based on a computer model developed by Nikolai Maximenko of the University of Hawaii and combines our knowledge of ocean currents and marine debris. It tells us that these new unnatural-natural systems are found in all our oceans. The northern and southern hemispheres of the oceans have different rubbish circulation systems. This is because they have separate circulating ocean currents. Called gyres, they rotate clockwise in the north, while in the south they turn anticlockwise. The North Atlantic Garbage Patch was first identified in 1972

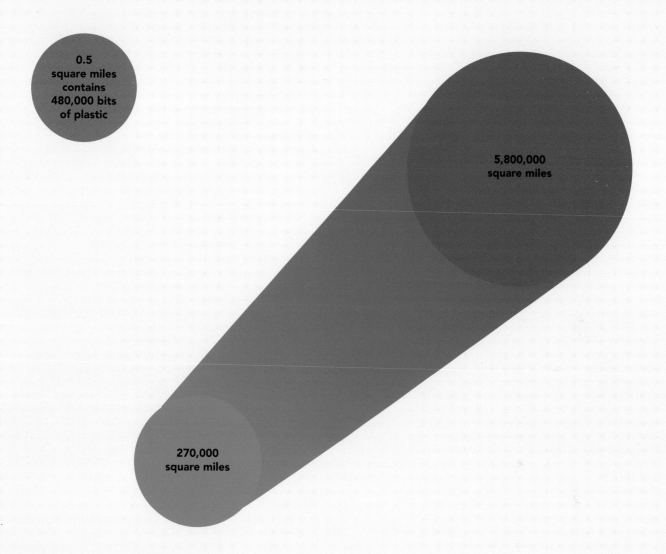

0.5
square miles
contains
480,000 bits
of plastic

5,800,000
square miles

270,000
square miles

Estimates of the extent of
the Pacific Trash Vortex.

and, like its cousins on other oceans, it isn't rooted to one spot but drifts about 1,000 miles (around 1,600km) across the course of a year.

Many solutions have been offered to remedy the problem of our rubbish-filled oceans. But the scale of the issue is so big, and its cause so far beyond the control of any one country, that neither the will nor the funds have yet been found to start cleaning up.

Theoretically we could scoop up this stuff and dispose of it (though how and where is another tricky question). It would be nice if world leaders could create a united front against this common menace. But for now, many scientists favour less dramatic and more low-tech solutions. The two key recommendations are simple: reduce our use of plastic, and stop throwing it away.

UNKNOWN OCEANS

Explored ocean

Unexplored ocean

Land

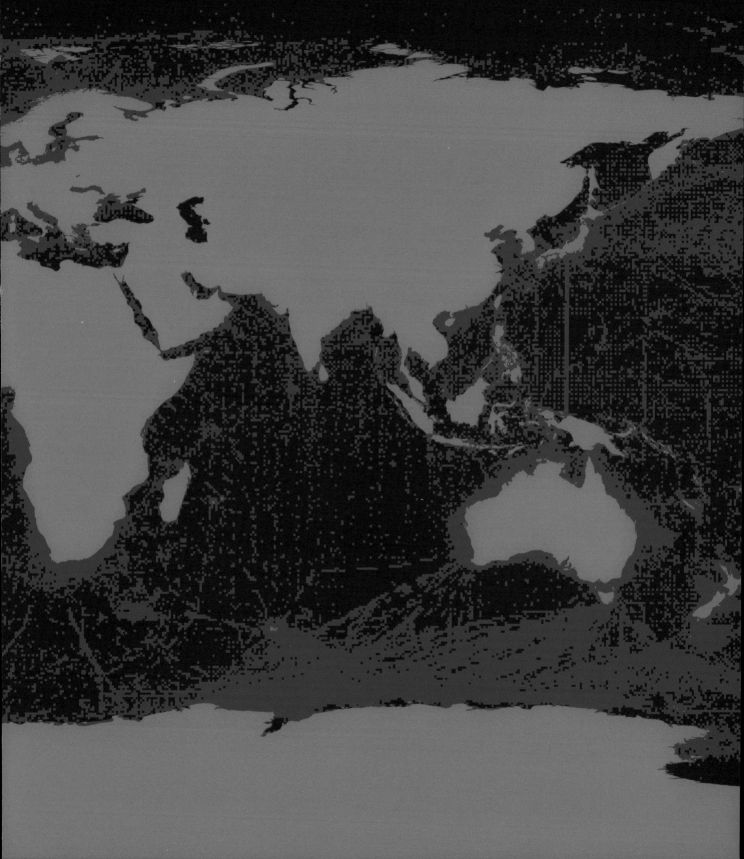

UNKNOWN OCEANS

What lives in the oceans is, for the most part, unknown. It may be a difficult fact to digest, but as this map proves, the areas in light blue show where we do have survey data; where marine life has been studied and identified. The dark blue areas are where we have little or no survey data. These vast zones cover the majority of the planet, including many coastal zones and lakes.

This map was released in late 2010 and is derived from the Census of Marine Life. It is the most wide-ranging census the planet has ever known: 2,700 scientists and 540 expeditions set out to itemise the life of the oceans. In so doing, they added considerably to our knowledge, finding 6,000 new species. Many of the discoveries are amazing: giant mats of microbes, which are now ranked among the earth's largest life forms; a shrimp that was thought to have become extinct 50 million years ago; and complex multicellular animals that exist without oxygen at the bottom of the sea. On a smaller scale, the census counted 38,000 different kinds of microbes in 2 pints (just over 1 litre) of seawater. It also confirmed that, excluding microbes, there are approximately 250,000 marine species currently known to science. There is a waiting list of about 750,000 other species that are on the radar but have yet to be described. There are, in addition, about a billion types of microbes in the oceans.

The gaps in our knowledge are considerable. The notion that we know more about the moon than we do about the deepest parts of the ocean is not hyperbole. There have been six different manned missions to the moon, but there have only been two crewed trips, down the almost 6 miles (11km) to the deepest part of the ocean, the Challenger Deep section of the Mariana Trench. The regions for which the marine census-takers tell us we have little data are, for the most part, not obscure corners. They reach far and wide. The sediments of the deep-ocean floor are hard to access, but they are one of the most species-rich marine habitats. Every expedition to the bottom of the deep ocean finds undescribed species, but there just haven't been that many expeditions, meaning that estimates of the number of species down there range wildly, from less than 1 million to 5 million.

250,000 Marine species currently
known to science

750,000 Estimated number of species
yet to be described

We are still a long way from having a comprehensive understanding of marine life. But it is only by being informed that we know how ignorant we are. Perhaps what the census has shown us most is just how much more there is to know.

DRAINING THE OCEANS

Drained area

Projection of 330ft (100m) drop
in ocean level

DRAINING THE OCEANS

Here we see what the world would look like if the level of the oceans fell by around 330ft (100m). In some ways it's a step back in time to before 10,000 BC, when a lot of the world's water was trapped in ice caps and glaciers and the water level was much lower. Back then Britain wasn't an island, and one could walk all the way across the North Sea. Archaeologists have been discovering the remains of spears and axes from beneath the North Sea, and have given the name 'Doggerland' to this drowned kingdom. The North Sea is not the only shallow sea, nor the only potential, and past, land bridge. After a 330ft (100m) fall in sea level, much of South East Asia becomes connected, and Papua New Guinea and Australia are joined into an even bigger island continent. We can also see that the land bridge which first allowed humans to enter the Americas from the north has returned, permitting direct passage through Siberia and into Alaska.

This projection is a frame taken from a sequence put together by NASA's National Geophysical Data Center. On one level, its appeal is simple. It's a fascinating insight into how varied and dramatic the hills and valleys of the oceans are. At 330ft (100m), this is one of the first images in NASA's set. It takes a while for some of the higher ridges that run down the middle of the great oceans to start cresting. These mid-ocean ranges – like the one that runs down the middle of the Atlantic – only start to appear at depths of 6,562 to 9,843ft (2,000m to 3,000m). You have to wait a long time for the oceans to be pretty much empty; that only happens at nearly 20,000ft (6,000m). Even then the really deep trenches are still full, the deepest of which is the Mariana Trench at nearly 36,000ft (10,911m).

Ocean levels are predicted to rise rather than fall. But the interest in looking at the reverse process – ocean draining – is not just wishful thinking. Once the ocean floor was cartographic terra incognita, but we are now starting to map it, just like the rest of the planet. Knowing the hills and valleys under the water is as necessary for oil-drillers and island-builders as it is for conservationists

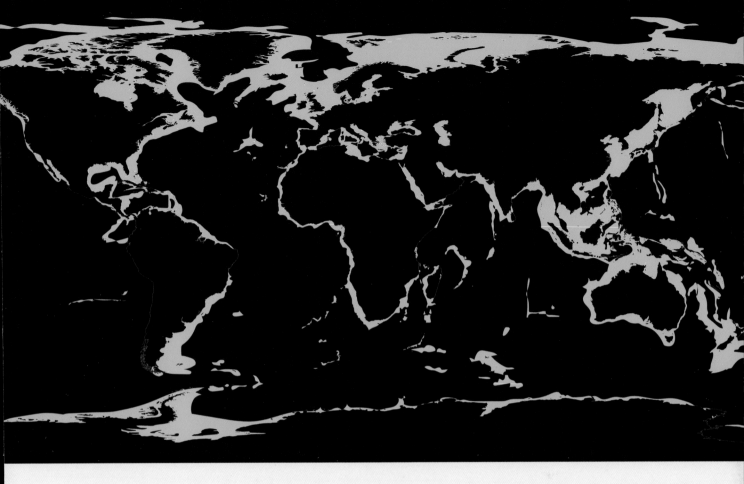

Map showing the Continental shelves and mid-ocean ridges which are revealed if the sea level decreased by 6,560ft (2,000m).

and marine scientists. Over the past few decades there has been a revolution in bathymetry, the study of underwater topography. Satellites have played a key role in this study. By measuring changes in the surface level of the ocean, US and European satellites map how the ocean responds to the gravitational pull of underwater features such as trenches and peaks. This data is now being used to create a new generation of underwater maps. The days when we could only map that fraction of the planet which is above sea level are gone.

DRIFTERS

- Australia
- Brazil
- Canada
- Chile
- China
- Europe-EUMETNET
- France
- India
- Indonesia
- Italy
- Japan
- Kenya
- Korea
- Mauritius
- Netherlands
- New Zealand
- Norway
- Peru
- Seychelles
- South Africa
- Spain
- UK
- USA-NOAA
- USA-other
- Unknown
- All other values

Participating countries and their contribution to the drifter programme

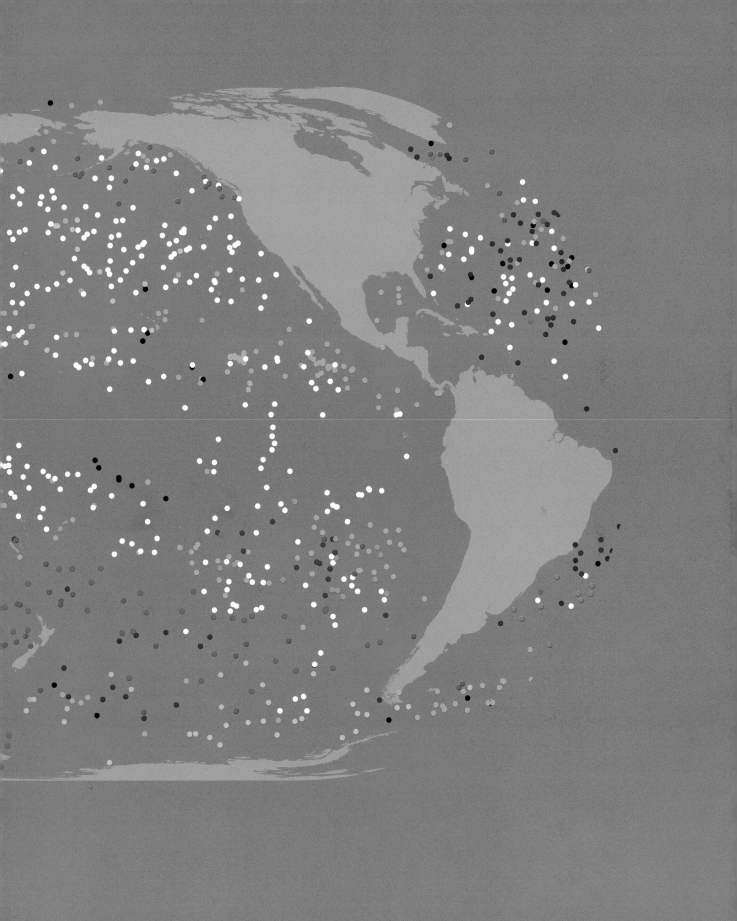

DRIFTERS

Drifters are seagoing buoys that take continuous measurements of water temperature as well as current speed, salinity and air pressure, and ping the results up to a satellite. This data is then fed back to earth, allowing anyone to check the location of individual drifters on constantly updated online maps. Although managed by the US government, the Global Drifter Program is an international effort, and this map gives us a recent snapshot of which buoys are being looked after by which of the programme's many partners and where they are. For example, we see buoys run by the Australian Bureau of Meteorology dotted across the Indian and Pacific oceans, and those belonging to the UK Met Office in the Atlantic. The US has the widest array, with a large number of devices in both the Pacific and the Atlantic Oceans.

The need for such an impressive flotilla of floating sensors has long been recognised by ocean researchers. An early model was put to sea in February 1979, and after a standardised and low-cost drifter had been developed, large-scale deployments began in 1988. Since then hundreds of buoys have been bobbing on the world's oceans, sending back information that has vastly expanded our knowledge of the seas. During the one-year period between September 2003 and August 2004, a total of 658 drifters were deployed by the US's National Oceanic and Atmospheric Administration, who manage the global programme: 440 from research vessels, 201 from vessels that participate in the Voluntary Observing Ship Program and 17 from the air. The goal of maintaining a network of 1,250 drifters, considered to be the number required for adequate coverage, was achieved on 18 September 2005.

The buoys are attached to a trailing sea anchor, which slows them down and stops them rushing too far off track. However, drifters often face a severe battering on the open sea, and lose their anchors, eventually washing up on shore, where they are stumbled upon by curious passers-by. The Global Drifter Program is very keen to monitor the whereabouts of all its fleet, including buoys that have gone missing in action. It instructs people who come across a lost buoy as follows: 'Look

1 Mauritius

2 Indonesia

26 Italy

85 Australia

130 France

380 **USA-NOAA**
(National Oceanic and
Atmospheric Administration)

Graphic showing the number of buoys in the ocean owned by five countries and the USA's National Oceanic and Atmospheric Administration (data accurate up until 20 March 2017).

for any identification [usually a five-digit number], or instructions on the surface of the float'; 'Take a picture of the drifter and all its components'; 'Contact "Drifter Webmaster" and send a picture and as much information as you can'.

In the future, more drifters will be sent into the least-known and less well-travelled parts of the oceans. There will also be dense deployments in the most complex and turbulent waters. New sensors are also expanding the range of features the buoys can measure, such as surface conductivity, rain rates, biochemical concentrations and the many ways in which the atmosphere and the seas interact.

LIGHTNING

0.1   75.0   150.00

Flashes per km² per year

<0.1

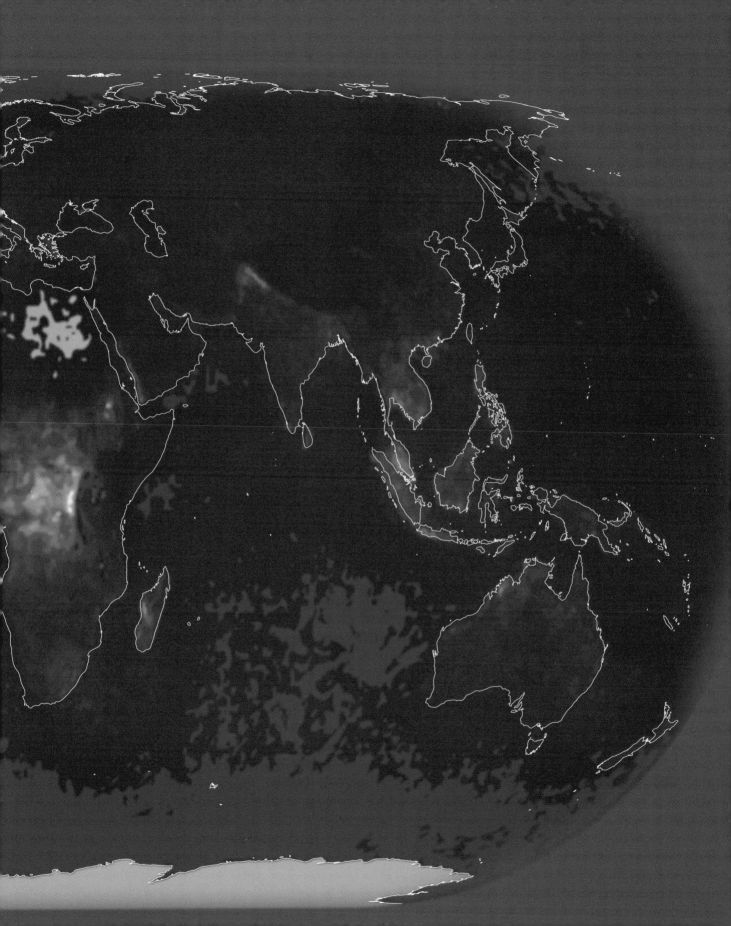

LIGHTNING

Across the oceans the sky remains dark and sombre, but on land and towards the Tropics it is rent with myriad tendrils of brilliant lightning. The skies of tropical Africa are more alive with lightning than anywhere else, with a particularly intense region of activity in the Eastern Congo. This map is based on the average lightning flashes per year per square kilometre for the years between 1995 and 2013. Places with the least lightning are grey and dark purple; they encompass both of the poles and all of the oceans, as well as much of the higher reaches of the northern hemisphere.

The lightning capital of the world is a disputed title. This map seems to support the claim of the small village of Kifuka in the mountains in the east of the Democratic Republic of the Congo, where 531 lightning strikes per square mile (205 lightning strikes per km^2) per year have been declared. However, recently Kifuka's position has been challenged on behalf of Lake Maracaibo in Venezuela, where 603 bolts per square mile (233 bolts per km^2) per year have been recorded. Either way it's a lot, especially when compared to the darker parts of the map, which have well below one flash per square kilometre per year.

Our planet sees about 40 to 50 flashes of lightning every second, which add up to around 1.4 billion flashes over the course of a year. There isn't much lightning over the sea because it doesn't heat up like the land. The land warms up relatively quickly and then gives off that heat, creating convection currents and atmospheric instability. Thus the thunderclouds you need for lightning are usually found over land. Since it's heat that drives this process, it also follows that the world's colder countries see less lightning.

The geography of lightning is not as arcane a topic as it might sound. Figures on the number of people killed by lightning range from 6,000 to 24,000 a year, but no one really knows the statistics. What is clear is that the poorest countries, in Africa and in Asia, have by far the most fatalities. Lightning has other devastating consequences, killing livestock, starting fires and causing surges through the electricity grid that destroy equipment and bring down the power supply.

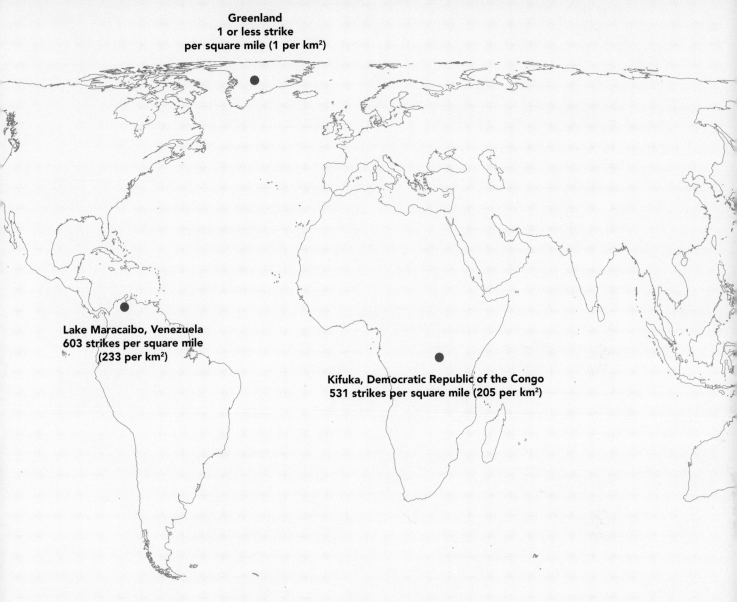

**Greenland
1 or less strike
per square mile (1 per km²)**

**Lake Maracaibo, Venezuela
603 strikes per square mile
(233 per km²)**

**Kifuka, Democratic Republic of the Congo
531 strikes per square mile (205 per km²)**

The two places with the highest level of lightning activity in comparison to Greenland, a far colder country and therefore one of the places where lightning is rare.

But there is another face to lightning. Across the brightly lit, pink parts of the map we find that lightning has an important role in traditional stories and indigenous religions. In many of these religions there are deities of lightning, served by priests and priestesses whose role it is to channel the dangerous but life-giving power of this seemingly magical force. For lightning is not looked on only as a bringer of death and destruction, but also as a harbinger of the rains.

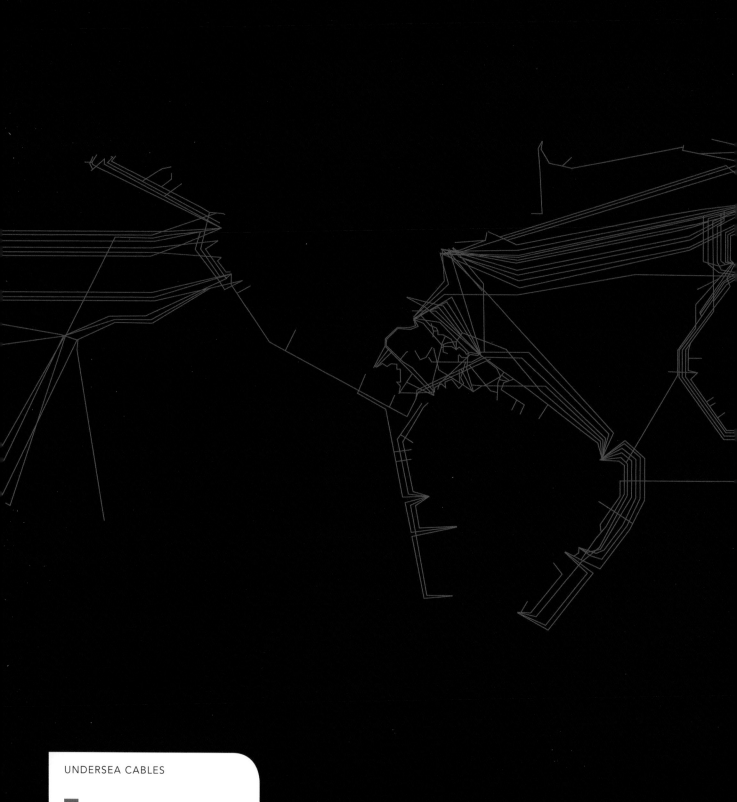

UNDERSEA CABLES

Cables

UNDERSEA CABLES

Although we are often told about the importance of satellites, and use such airy concepts as 'the Cloud' to talk about data storage, it is underwater cables that are the modern world's key communication devices. They carry nearly all of our global Internet traffic. The map may look as if it's covered with them, but in fact, given what they do, there are remarkably few. About 300 cable systems carry almost all the world's transoceanic data. This map shows how all of the continents, apart from Antarctica, are now connected by undersea communications cables, as well as the density of connections in East and South East Asia and in the North Atlantic. Less populated, or less developed, areas have fewer cables, as can be seen from the lack of connectivity to Western Australia and Bangladesh.

Undersea communication is not a new concept. In 1842 Samuel Morse sent a telegraph signal through a wire cable he'd wrapped in tarred hemp and rubber and strung out into the waters of New York Harbor. The first transatlantic cable was laid in 1866; a cable connecting India to Yemen in 1870. Recent decades have witnessed a revolution in the industry in terms of both the types and the amount of data that can be sent. Old-style cables were laid just point-to-point. These days submarine branching units allow a single cable to connect to multiple destinations. The first transatlantic fibre-optic cable went live in 1988.

The modern demand for undersea cables reflects the fact that they offer a much better and bigger signal than satellites. Not only are the speeds much faster, but cables can communicate tens of terabytes of data per second, vastly more than any satellite. The cables use light to encode information and can send data at speeds approaching the speed of light. They are also much more hard-wearing than satellites. Cables are unaffected by weather and are very resilient. In recent years demand has outstripped supply. Only when capacity undersea is reached do telecommunications companies switch to satellites as a standby.

If you wanted to disrupt world communications, it would make much more sense to cut through one of these cables than to try to knock out a satellite. The International Cable Protection Committee was set up in 1958 to work out ways

300

About 300 cable systems
carry almost all of the world's
transoceanic data.

of keeping the system safe. Today cables at shore end are armoured with steel and often buried. In the deep sea protection is provided by their remoteness. But that factor also means that they are difficult to repair. It's not so much a matter of sabotage that threatens to bring down the system but faults, of which there are many each year, as well as the odd gnawing shark.

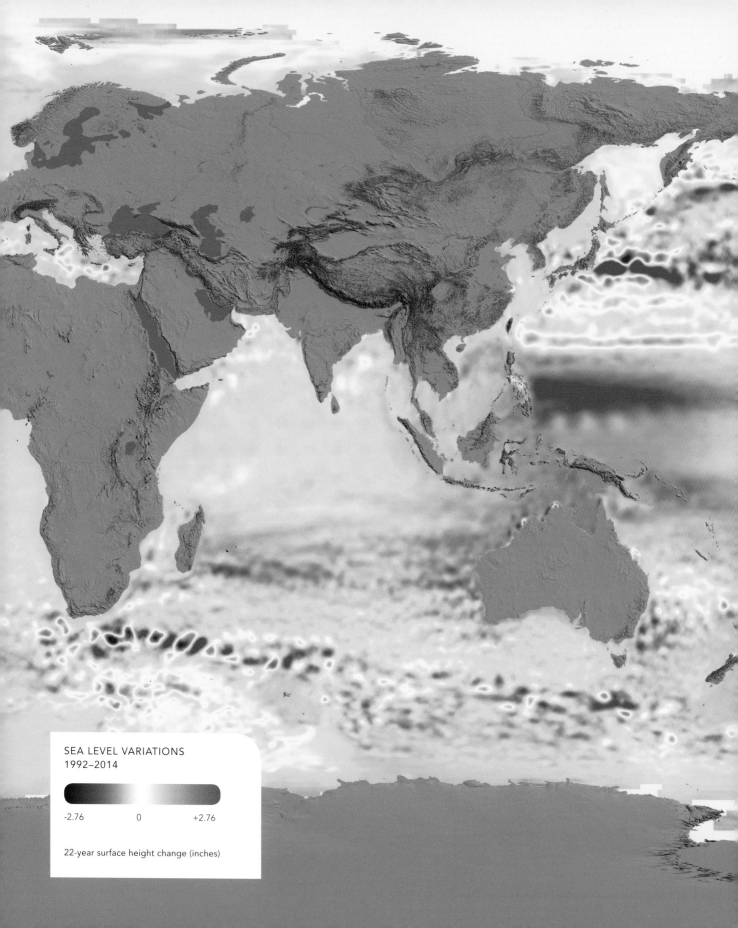

SEA LEVEL VARIATIONS
1992–2014

-2.76   0   +2.76

22-year surface height change (inches)

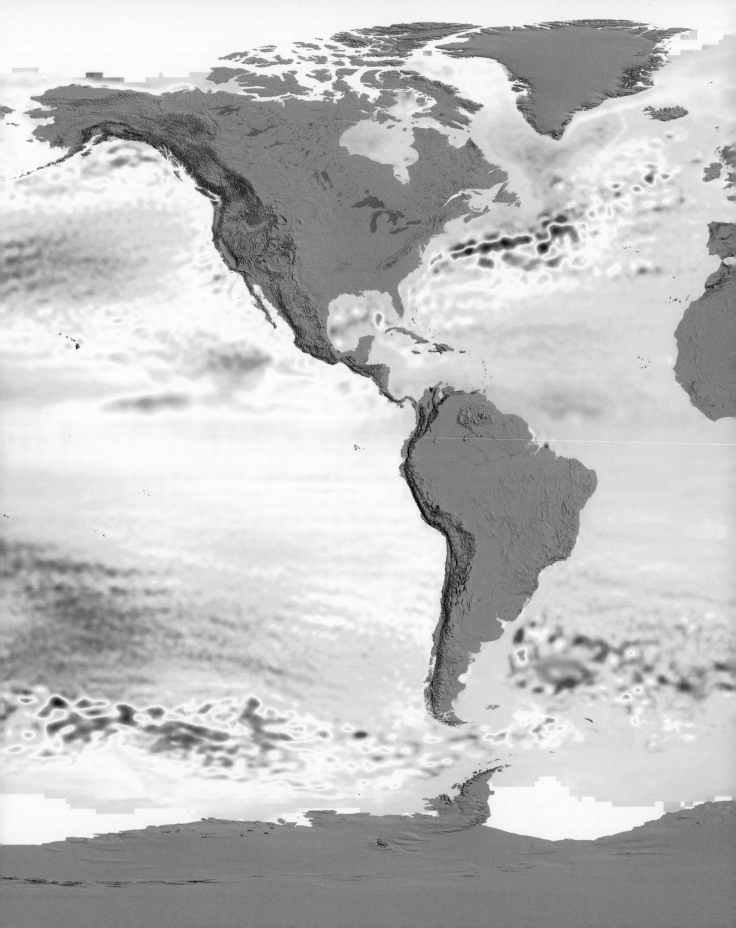

SEA LEVEL VARIATIONS

Since 1992, seas around the world have risen by an average of nearly 3in (about 7.5cm), but that increase has not been uniform. The overall trend is global, but local sea level changes also matter. We've long been familiar with the idea that the sea is a flat, featureless surface, but we need to get used to thinking about it as a mobile and fast-moving range of heights and depths. We're not talking about watery Everests, of course; this NASA visualisation records falls and rises of between -2.75in (-7cm) and +2.75in (+7cm) – the measured data actually extends above and below these limits. These may sound like tiny numbers, but millions of people live in low-lying areas where even the smallest rise can mean the difference between safety and inundation.

The mapping of water heights is a new area for cartographers. It presents huge challenges. The variations are small and continually on the move. This sea level data was collected by a number of different satellites, and compiles information gathered between 1992 and 2014. Introducing it, NASA's Tom Wagner explains that 'the ocean has topography. You can almost think of it like a mountain range with peaks and valleys.' He adds that the 'coast of California is a little bit of a valley right now, and this is caused by a combination of wind and ocean currents'. Wagner tells us that there are two main causes for the overall rise in sea level. One is well known: the water released by melting ice sheets and glaciers. But half of the rise is explained by another factor, which is that as the planet warms, so do the seas, and, since warm things expand, the volume of the oceans has grown, causing sea level rise.

Given that warmer water expands and colder water contracts, these patches of colour also provide an indication of temperature changes. Moreover, since cold water is more saline and warm water less so, it is a map of the sea's changing geography of its saltiness. But it is the way the map shows variation in the height of the seas which has really grabbed people's attention. It is particularly striking that, in the western Pacific Ocean, winds and ocean currents have piled up warm water. This Pacific bulge suggests that the crowded coastal communities found

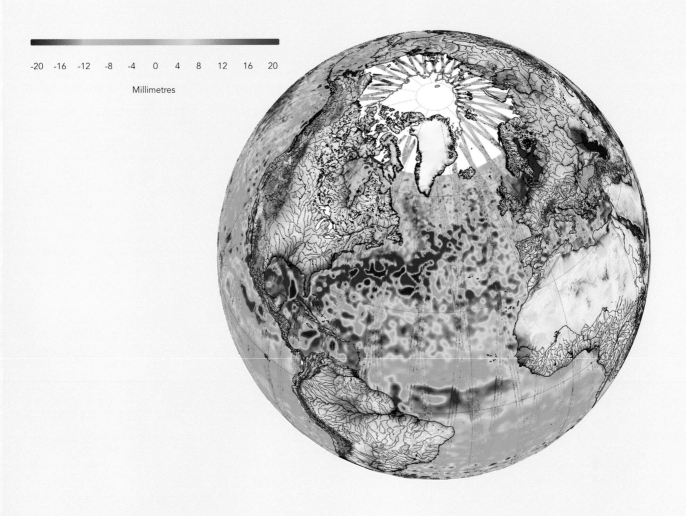

-20 -16 -12 -8 -4 0 4 8 12 16 20

Millimetres

Satellite image showing the variations in sea level when sea ice reached a historic low during September 2012.

throughout South East Asia may be more at risk than was previously thought. Other danger areas lie in the Southern Ocean and high North Atlantic, but the smaller coastal populations in these regions suggest that our attention should be focused on the hundreds of millions of people living in low-lying areas of countries such as the Philippines.

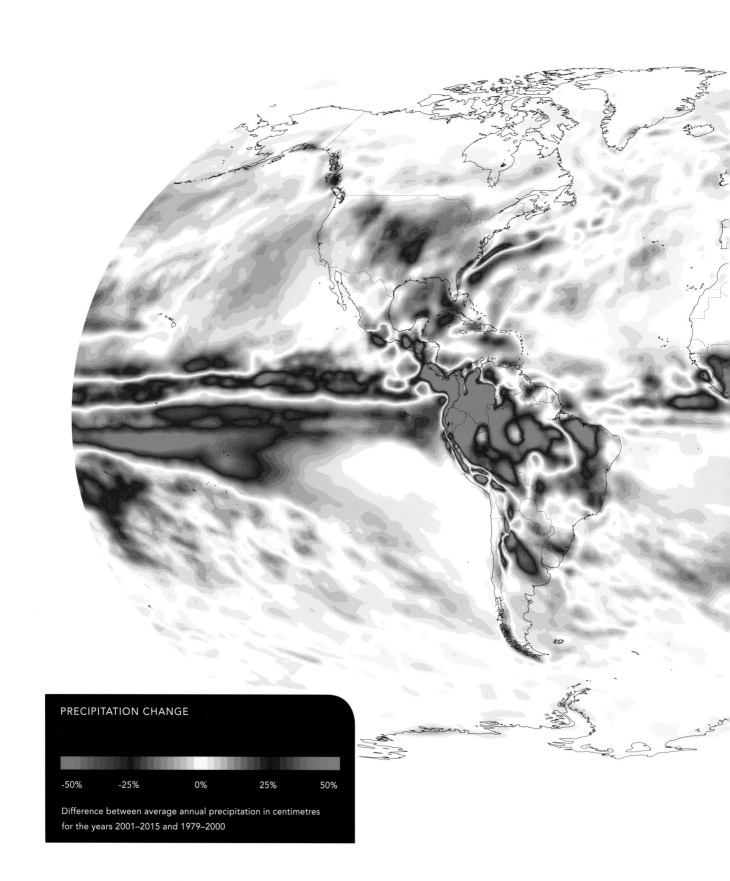

PRECIPITATION CHANGE

-50%   -25%   0%   25%   50%

Difference between average annual precipitation in centimetres
for the years 2001–2015 and 1979–2000

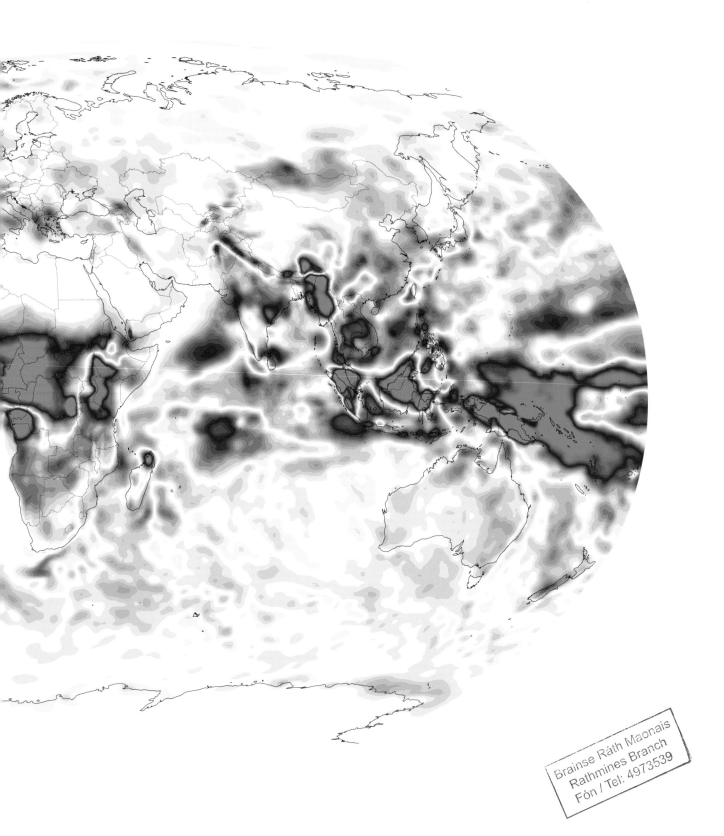

PRECIPITATION CHANGE

Climate change has made us a planet of weather-watchers. A warming world sounds like it will mean a drier planet, and for many it will. The dark oranges and misty browns on this map are places that have become drier. They are vast; great sweeps of North America, Europe and Asia, as well as the southern oceans and Australasia, are having less rain and snow. But an equally striking aspect of this map is the unevenness and turbulence it shows, especially in the tropics. This is where much of the drama is. Big patches of South America and South East Asia are getting a lot more rain, but these wet zones are cheek by jowl with regions that are becoming drier. A worrying and striking feature is the large and populous Sub-Saharan region shown here in deep orange – a part of Africa that is suffering long-term drought.

This is a map that looks at the difference between the average annual precipitation for the years 2001–15 and the years 1979–2000. It is derived from data supplied by the European Centre for Medium-Range Weather Forecasts. The map shows recent changes, but longer-term studies have also concluded that many tropical areas are significantly wetter or drier than they were a century ago.

Going closer into the map, particular stories unfold. Let's look at Mali. Here the Sahara desert is expanding southward every year. The north of Mali, a landlocked West African country of fourteen million people, has suffered drought in its northern desert for decades, but more recently the lower and, traditionally, more fertile and wetter third of the country has lost more than half its yearly rainfall. The consequences are not just humanitarian but also political. Drought has created a desperate generation and pushed whole communities off their land and into conflict with their neighbours, leaving the country more vulnerable to exploitation by extremists.

There has always been a lot of rain in some parts of the tropics. The wettest place in the world is the village of Mawsynram in India, which gets almost 468in (11,871mm) of rain a year, compared to the UK's almost 35in (885mm). Having rain is nearly always better than doing without it, and Mawsynram knows how

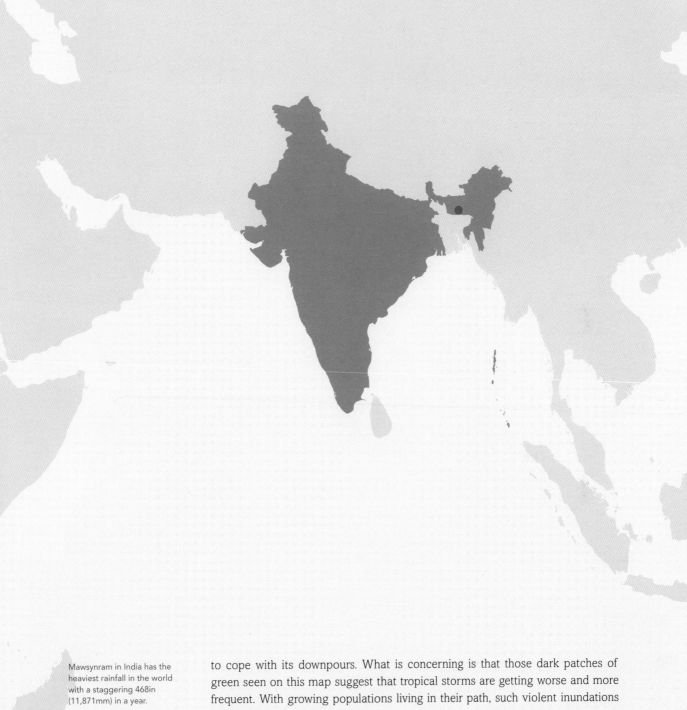

Mawsynram in India has the heaviest rainfall in the world with a staggering 468in (11,871mm) in a year.

to cope with its downpours. What is concerning is that those dark patches of green seen on this map suggest that tropical storms are getting worse and more frequent. With growing populations living in their path, such violent inundations can have disastrous consequences.

Here is a map that is not just about the facts and figures of rainfall. It's a map of human survival and social crisis in a rapidly changing world.

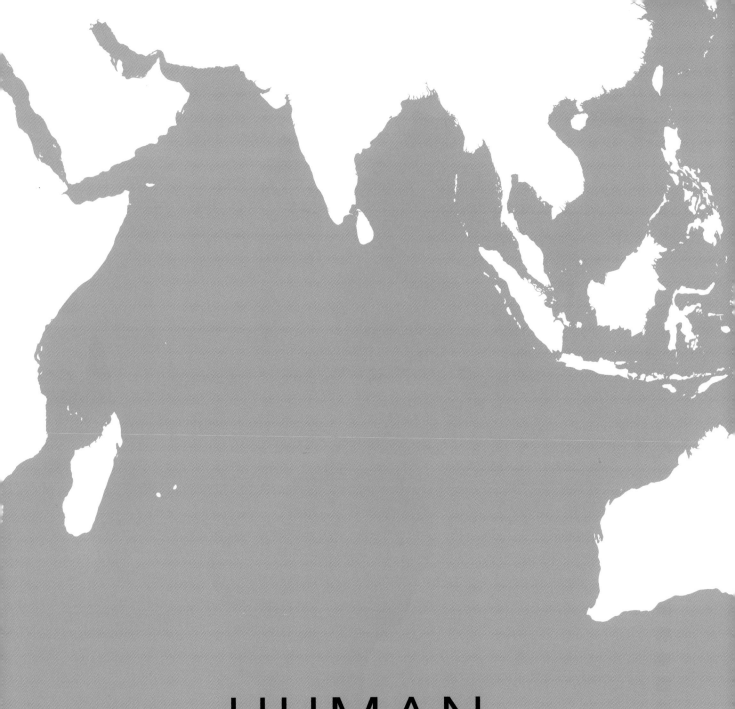

HUMAN
AND ANIMAL

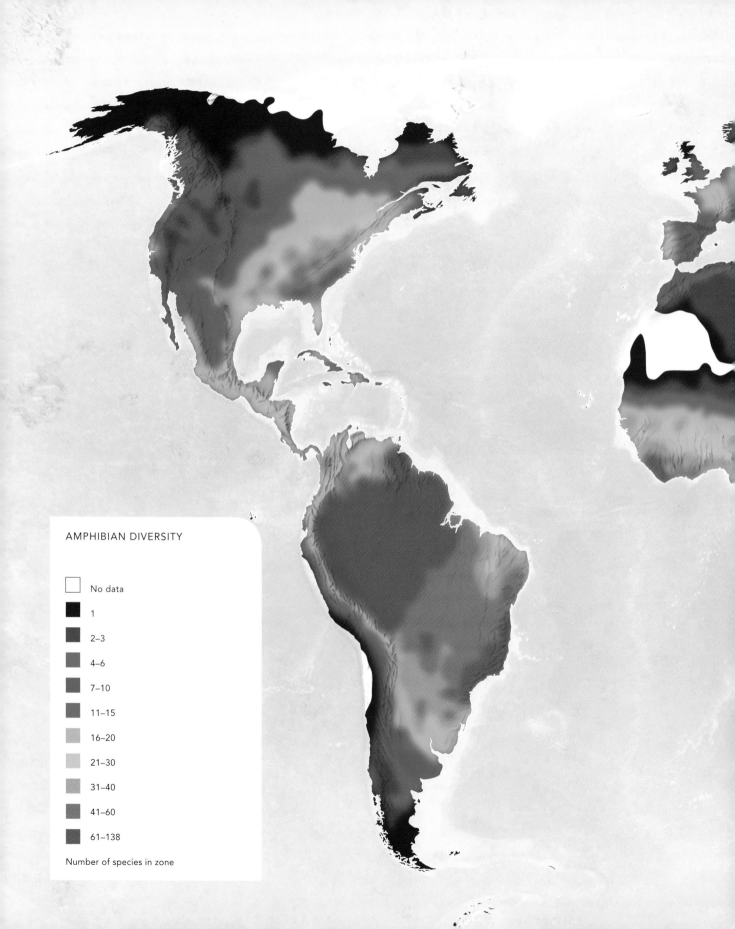

AMPHIBIAN DIVERSITY

No data

1

2–3

4–6

7–10

11–15

16–20

21–30

31–40

41–60

61–138

Number of species in zone

AMPHIBIAN DIVERSITY

Amphibians are incredibly varied. They come in outrageous colours, from electric blue to emerald green, and have a corresponding diversity of eccentric behaviours. There are around 6,000 known species, and new ones are still being found. Frogs, toads, newts, salamanders and other amphibians are unique, because nearly every one of them undergoes metamorphosis, breaking their body down and changing from a tadpole into an adult. They also need access to both land and water: a wet habitat is important to their survival. Habitat loss is the main reason why almost half of all amphibian species are in severe decline. There are nearly as many threatened species of amphibian as the number of threatened birds and mammals combined.

This map is based on the Global Amphibian Assessment, which drew together more than 500 scientists from over 60 countries and provided a global picture of this conservation challenge. The importance of protecting habitat in the tropics, especially its rainforest environments, is stark. The reason tropical rainforests are crowded with so many types of amphibian is, in part, a reflection of their warm, humid climate, but also the fact that they are the oldest major habitat on earth – there has been plenty of time for their inhabitants to diversify. The size of the tropical belt around the world is also significant, since large distances within a single habitat encourage 'speciation'. Speciation is the evolutionary process of splitting up into species. It has been theorised that another reason speciation is so evident in the South American and African tropics is that previous periods of high sea level created isolated islands within these regions, each of which developed its own 'native' species.

Unsurprisingly, the country with the largest number of amphibians is Brazil. The US is a similar size to Brazil but has fewer than half its variety. Much smaller-scale contrasts can also be picked out from the map. For example, Britain has only seven native species whilst other West European countries have several times that number.

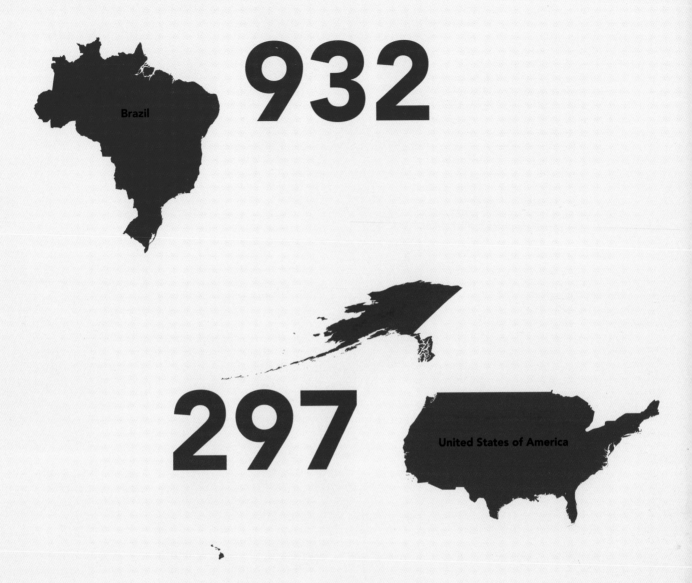

932

Brazil

297

United States of America

Despite being a similar size, the US has under a third of the number of amphibian species to Brazil.

Amphibians are very sensitive to environmental change. Living on land and in water means that they need two kinds of habitat to survive. If you want to help your local frogs and newts thrive, just conserving ponds will not, unfortunately, be enough. Like other amphibians, they spend most of their lives out of water and can roam over large areas. The fact that amphibian eggs are shell-less and the adults have very thin skin also makes them vulnerable. Pollutants impact them quickly and severely, as do increases in ultraviolet radiation which occur as a result of reductions in the level of atmospheric ozone. As their variety shows, these remarkable and beautiful creatures are an evolutionary success story, but today amphibians face the prospect of mass extinction.

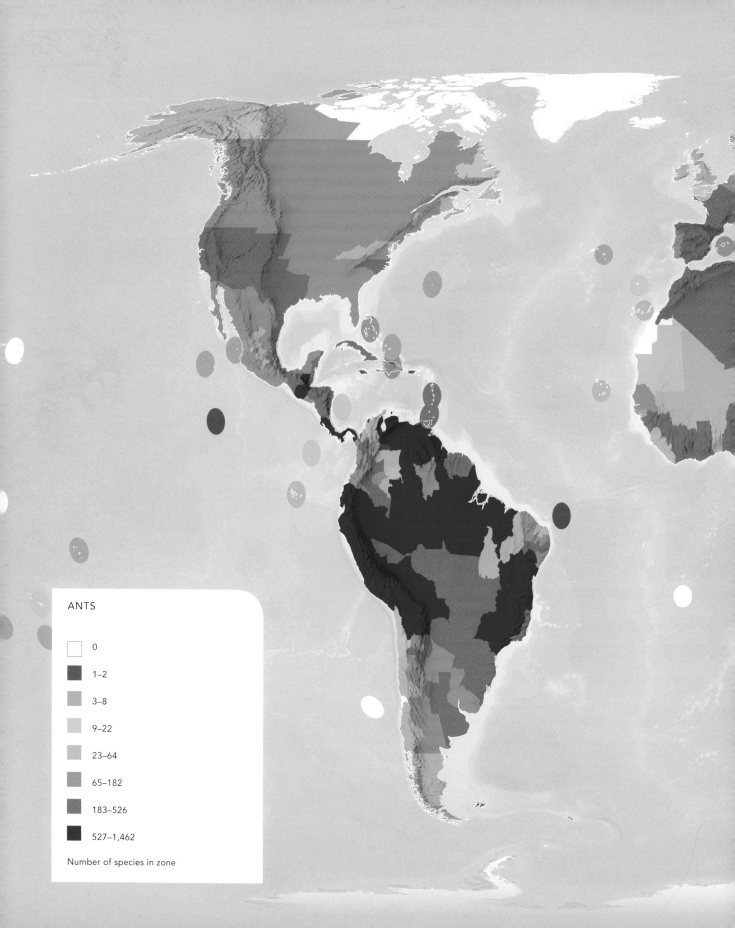

ANTS

☐ 0

■ 1–2

■ 3–8

■ 9–22

■ 23–64

■ 65–182

■ 183–526

■ 527–1,462

Number of species in zone

ANTS

To date, 12,500 species of ant have been identified, although it is thought there are thousands more waiting to be catalogued. The variety is most apparent in the hottest parts of the world. Our map's dark reds, in South America, much of Africa, South East Asia and Australia show us that temperature is the single best predictor of ant species density. The blue areas have just a few varieties, but the deepest red area is home for up to 1,462 species.

Ants in the Tropics come in all sizes, from the world's smallest, which are about a millimetre long, to the largest, such as *Dinoponera gigantea*, an alarming Amazonian ant that reaches almost 2in (4cm) in length. One study of a single jungle tree in Peru identified 43 species of ant; another of a single tree in Borneo found 61 species. These are impressive numbers, especially when one considers that there are just over 60 species found across the entire British Isles.

This map offers both a national and a regional picture of ant species, with the biggest countries being broken up into states and provinces to allow a more detailed view. We can see how the warmer Southern States of the US have far more ant species than further north. It is based on the work of the Global Ant Biodiversity Informatics project, which aims to create a single database incorporating and mapping every ant species. It is led by Evan Economo of the Okinawa Institute of Science and Technology in Japan and Benoit Guénard of the Insect Biodiversity and Biogeography Laboratory at the University of Hong Kong. Their cartographic subject matter is almost overwhelming in its abundance and plurality. Ants are one of the planet's most numerous insects, with an estimated total population of about one quadrillion (1,000,000,000,000,000), and constitute at least 15 per cent of the world's land-based animal biomass.

Understanding ant diversity and geography is important because ants, apart from being one of the most successful creatures on earth, are also one of its most vital. Ants remove a lot of the decaying and dead matter that would otherwise surround us, and are a source of food for many other animals higher up the food chain. They perform other, less well-known services too. Ants improve the soil,

61

United Kingdom

France

224

Italy

253

South Africa

683

62  **Finland**

The number of ant species in five countries, showing a greater diversity in hotter zones than cold.

allowing better water infiltration and increasing the levels of oxygen and nitrogen, which means that ants are often needed for good harvests. One study found that ants and termites increased wheat crop yields in arid climates by 36 per cent.

They are also biological control agents, preying on many pest insects. Edward O. Wilson, the renowned biologist who spent much of his career studying ants, concluded that if the world's invertebrates were to disappear, 'I doubt the human species would last more than a few months', adding, 'the truth is we need the invertebrates but they don't need us'. In any list of creatures that human life depends upon, the ant would be near the top.

BIRD DIVERSITY

Low diversity   High diversity

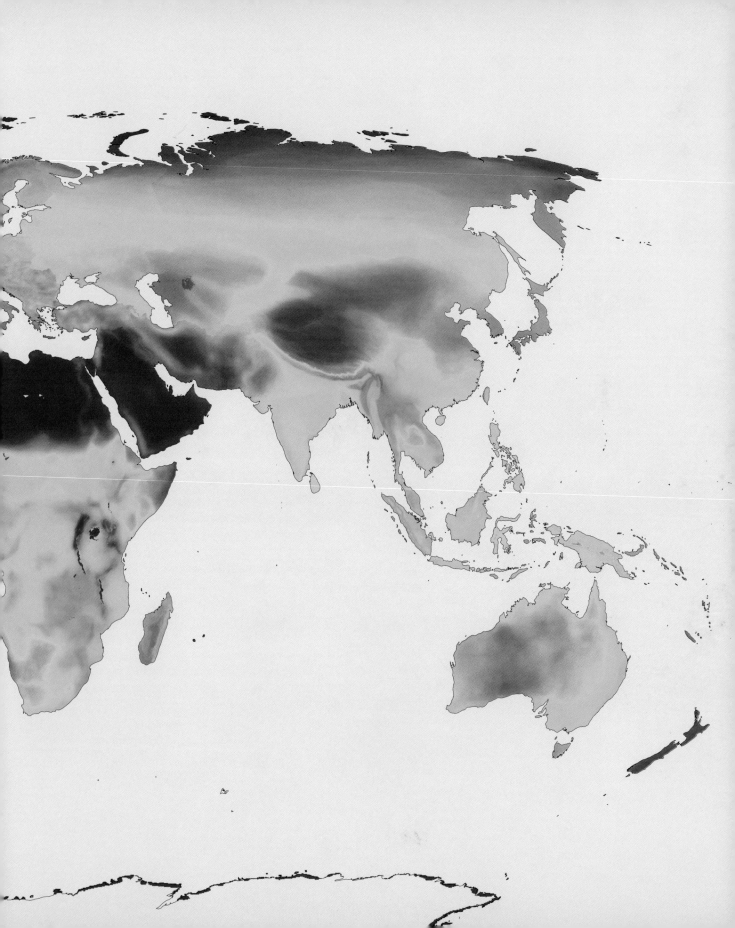

BIRD DIVERSITY

There are 112,665 species included in this planetary overview of bird diversity: from number one, the Ostrich, all the way down to number 112,665, the Tsingy Wood-rail. We see immediately that variety is much thinner across the colder and/or drier reaches of the northern hemisphere. By contrast, the explosions of light and dark rust seen in South East Asia, Sub-Saharan Africa and across much of South America tell us where to go to find birds of every size, shape and colour. It's also evident that there are many hot spots within the tropics: the Amazon Basin and the Tropical Andes have terrific variety, as does the region around Lake Victoria in Africa.

The map is based on work carried out by BirdLife International and NatureServe, and provides a compelling picture of just how valuable certain parts of the planet are as nature reserves. BirdLife International point out that not only do most tropical regions have an incredible variety of birds, but also that tropical birds 'tend to have smaller ranges, so that the actual species found vary more from place to place'. They also pick out other interesting patterns, linking high rainfall rates to greater species diversity, as well as specific findings: among seabirds, for example, the greatest diversity is at mid-latitude in the southern hemisphere.

Bird diversity is a good indicator of more general patterns of species richness and environmental change. Birds are easy to observe; most are active by day and can be seen from a distance. So our picture of birds, although it is unlikely to be 100 per cent, is more complete than for most other creatures. This means bird diversity can be used as a barometer for other fluctuations: decline and change in the distribution of birds usually reflect wider patterns of decline and change. BirdLife International have identified 10,000 'Important Bird Areas' in almost two hundred countries. In East Africa, the 228 Important Bird Areas in Ethiopia, Kenya, Tanzania and Uganda contain 97 per cent of the region's 97 endemic mammals, 90 per cent of 80 globally threatened mammals and 92 per cent of 131 endemic snakes and amphibians.

24
Critically endangered

169
Globally threatened

49
Endangered

96
Vulnerable

The status of bird species in Brazil – the South American country has the highest number of globally threatened species in the world.

Looking at bird diversity is not just about liking birds; it is about a much wider interest in biodiversity. And although bird variety is much greater in the tropics, there are still plenty of rich habitats in the colder north. Indeed, Britain has 313 designated Important Bird Areas, a figure that reflects not only the number of keen birdwatchers and conservers, but also the fact that you don't need to travel to Africa or South America to find spectacular birdlife.

COUNTRIES WITH THE
LARGEST NUMBER OF
VENOMOUS ANIMALS

<10

10–20

20–30

30–40

40–50

>50

No data

Number of venomous species in zone

COUNTRIES WITH THE LARGEST NUMBER OF VENOMOUS ANIMALS

There is only one venomous species in Britain: the viper. But Mexico has 80, Brazil 79, Australia 66 and Colombia, India, Indonesia and Vietnam each have more than 50. That there are so few in some places but so many in others is largely a reflection of the fact that the Tropics have a far greater diversity of nearly all species. Another reason is that many venomous creatures are cold-blooded, like snakes, and prefer hot environments. These explanations also point to the fact that countries tend to have more of these deadly creatures in their warmest states.

As is often the case with nature, there remain some mysteries. For example, why are there more venomous insects in Australia than in other hot countries? Another head-scratcher is why the US has nearly the same number of venomous species as tropical Africa. At least one mystery is easily solved. It appears from this map that France is far more venomous than its neighbouring countries, but this is a consequence of the way the data combines France with its South American territory of French Guiana.

The data for this map is drawn from the Living Hazards Database kept by the US's Armed Forces Pest Management Board. It ranges across more than 500 species worldwide; species which inject venom and 'are reported to cause serious injury or death of humans'. Filling this definition are mainly snakes, spiders and scorpions. There is also a 'miscellaneous others' category, which includes reptiles like Gila monsters and some surprisingly deadly seashells. My favourite is the Geographic Cone Snail, found on Indian and Pacific Ocean reefs. The Living Hazards Database informs us that this creature, much prized for its mottled shell, is almost unbelievably deadly: 'the human lethal dose for its venom has been estimated at just 0.029–0.038mg for every kilogram of body mass; 65 per cent of human stinging cases are fatal without medical attention – although only 36 such fatalities have been recorded since 1670.'

The world's most venomous animal is the Box jellyfish, which floats in coastal waters off Northern Australia and throughout the Indo-Pacific. It has caused

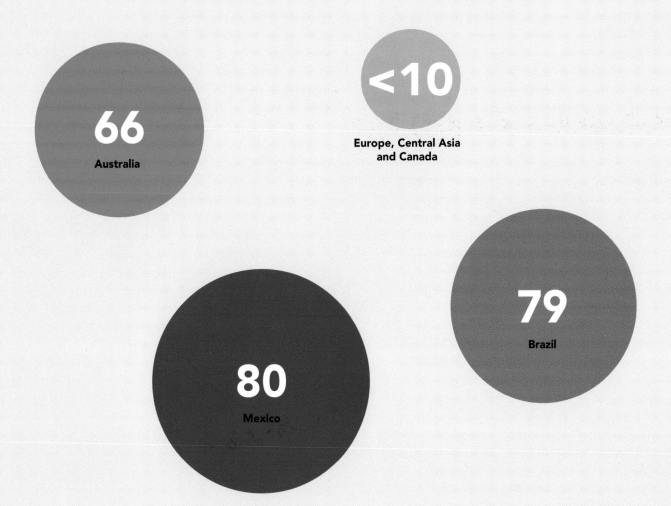

66
Australia

<10
Europe, Central Asia
and Canada

80
Mexico

79
Brazil

Whilst Mexico, Brazil and Australia are home to numerous venomous animals, countries in Europe and Central Asia have fewer than ten on average.

thousands of deaths over the past fifty years – its venom is so strong that human victims usually go straight into shock and so drown or die of heart failure.

The snake is the creature that most commonly causes harm, though. Research carried out in 2008 calculated that globally there were anywhere between 20,000 and 94,000 snakebite deaths each year. Southern Asia is the region with the highest fatality level, with India suffering 11,000 deaths alone, more than any other country in the world.

Before we imagine ourselves at war with these species, it is worth remembering that it is they, not us, that are in danger of extinction. Moreover, the expansion of human settlement and the absence of adequate healthcare are better explanations for the human fatalities that occur than demonising animals, which, for the most part, just want to be left well alone.

NEGLECTED TROPICAL
DISEASES

1 NTD present

2 NTDs present

3 NTDs present

4 NTDs present

>5 NTDs present

NEGLECTED TROPICAL DISEASES

Tropical diseases are thriving. Often deadly, vicious, yet in many cases treatable once contracted, most rarely hit the headlines.

They are called 'neglected tropical diseases' because they tend to be overshadowed by the 'big three': HIV/AIDS, tuberculosis and malaria, which attract the majority of the funding. Many of the lesser-known diseases have a social stigma attached to them and impact the poorest people in the poorest nations, especially those without adequate sanitation and who live in close contact with infected water sources and livestock. They include leprosy, rabies, trachoma and dengue fever as well as parasitic conditions such as guinea-worm disease, Chagas disease, echinococcosis and 'river blindness'. These diseases have been largely wiped out in richer countries, and have not attracted much attention from the leading drug companies because there is little profit to be made from their cure.

This, then, is a map of poverty but also of inadequate sanitation and healthcare provision. Neglected tropical diseases often occur together, and Africa is illuminated brightly on this map as a continent plagued by multiple forms of these diseases. Latin America and nearly all of Asia are also badly affected. The World Health Organisation estimates that neglected tropical diseases affect more than one billion people – one-sixth of the world's population – and kill 534,000 people worldwide every year.

And yet these are also some of the cheapest and simplest diseases to treat. The cost of treatment for most neglected tropical diseases drug programmes is less than fifty cents (US) per person, per year, with treatments often as straightforward as taking a course of deworming tablets. One of the best places medication can be administered is within schools. School attendance is closely linked to the battle against neglected tropical diseases. Studies show that children stay longer at schools that deliver drug programmes, but without such programmes many fail to progress in or to complete their education. Deworming not only decreases school absenteeism by 25 per cent, but increases adult earnings by 20 per cent.

1

Neglected tropical diseases affect more than one billion people – one-sixth of the world's population

Launched in 2012, the London Declaration on Neglected Tropical Diseases brought together many international agencies with the aim of wiping out ten of the worst of these diseases by 2020. Pharmaceutical companies are trying to salvage their reputations by contributing to this effort. In 2015 they donated enough tablets for 1.5 billion treatments. One of the key primary goals of the London Declaration is to literally map out the problem. Finding out which areas suffer from which outbreaks is essential to the task of combating disease; when it comes to human health, maps are on the front line. To take one example, the Global Trachoma Mapping Project mapped a total of 1,627 districts in 29 countries and identified 100 million people who are at risk from trachoma blindness, doubling the population already known to require intervention against trachoma – approximately half of whom live in Ethiopia, which has one of the highest rates of prevalence for the disease in the world.

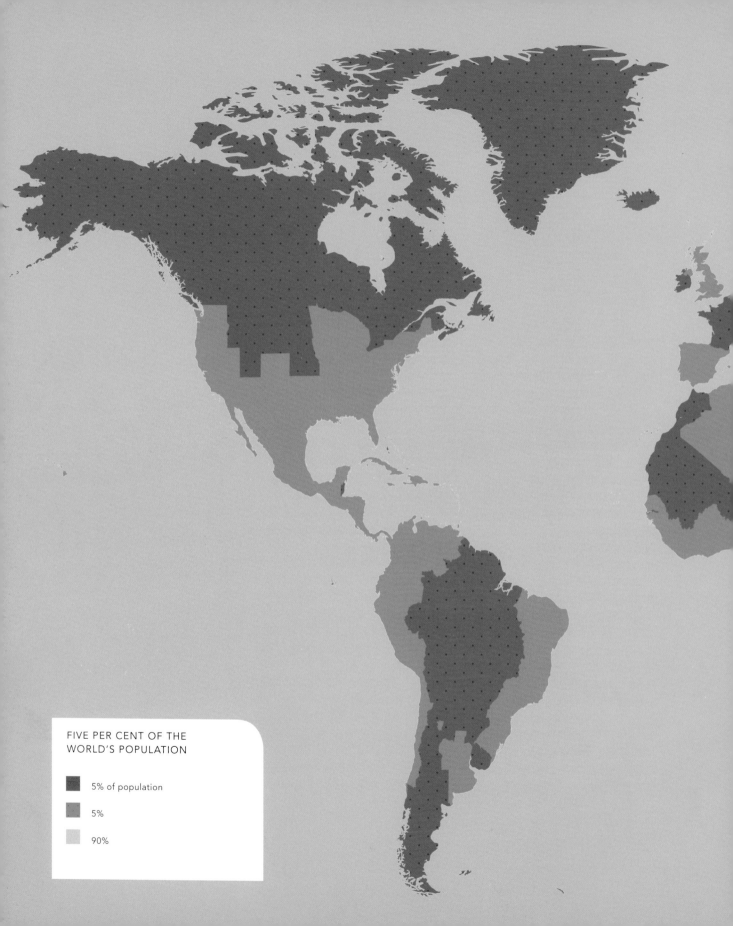

FIVE PER CENT OF THE
WORLD'S POPULATION

- 5% of population
- 5%
- 90%

FIVE PER CENT OF THE WORLD'S POPULATION

Can you name all the territories in green? Or the states in red? If you succeed, then each answer will contain five per cent of the world's population. I'd be impressed if you can: it's a bit of a trick question. The red patch includes three states in India – Bihar, Jharkhand and West Bengal – as well as Bangladesh. The green also contains a mixture of nations and local states; that's why it dips down into the middle of the US and skirts away from the coasts of South America. The green is scooping together many of the world's least-populated places, although it does also include some relatively densely settled nations, such as France. The red and green provide us not only with an odd contrast and combination of places, but also a fascinating way of grasping how unevenly the world's population is distributed. Clearly it is very concentrated indeed around the Bay of Bengal.

This map is derived from the work of a New York-based map enthusiast, Max Galka. He found a version online and honed it down into its current form. Thousands of great maps are being created every year in the same way, bubbling up from below. As is true for Wikipedia, an initial scepticism usually gives way to admiration. Not only are many of these maps carefully done, accurate and thoughtful, but they are usually surrounded by a lively debate and links that invite you 'to play with the data yourself'.

Max's commentary is a case in point. 'What I find most interesting,' he says, 'is that such a dense population centre can be in an area that has so little global prominence.' He's also interested in how different people read the map: 'many people seem to view the map from the perspective of overpopulation/ overcrowding, or as a political message about inequality between the developed and the developing world'. I'm not sure how anyone could see this map as offering a contrast between the 'developed' and 'developing' world, but I certainly saw it through the prism of overpopulation. The population of Bangladesh in 2016 was a little over 164 million, and the three East India states add another 230 million or so. Those kinds of numbers in such a small, low-lying and flood-prone area must be a risk for human health and catastrophic for the environment.

**Bangladesh
164 million**

**Tokelau
1,293**

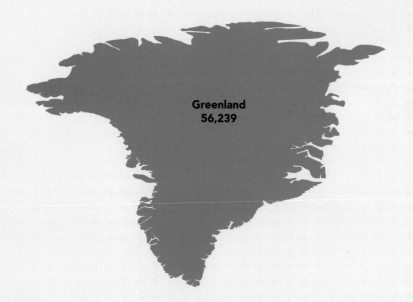

**Greenland
56,239**

The crowded and the uncrowded.

But Max offers another, more optimistic assessment: 'I see South Asia's dense population as a positive thing,' he writes. 'It is very efficient economically, socially and environmentally for people to live in dense population centres', adding that the map 'tells me that the economic opportunities of living with lots of people outweigh the problems'. With rising urbanisation, understanding the reasons behind Max's optimism could be crucial.

ECOLOGICAL FOOTPRINT
PER CAPITA

0.000000

0.000001–0.920000

0.920001–1.260000

1.260001–1.600000

1.600001–1.910000

1.910001–2.760000

2.760001–3.530000

3.530001–4.400000

4.400001–5.740000

5.740001–9.570000

EFpC = natural resources consumed by a
nation divided by its population

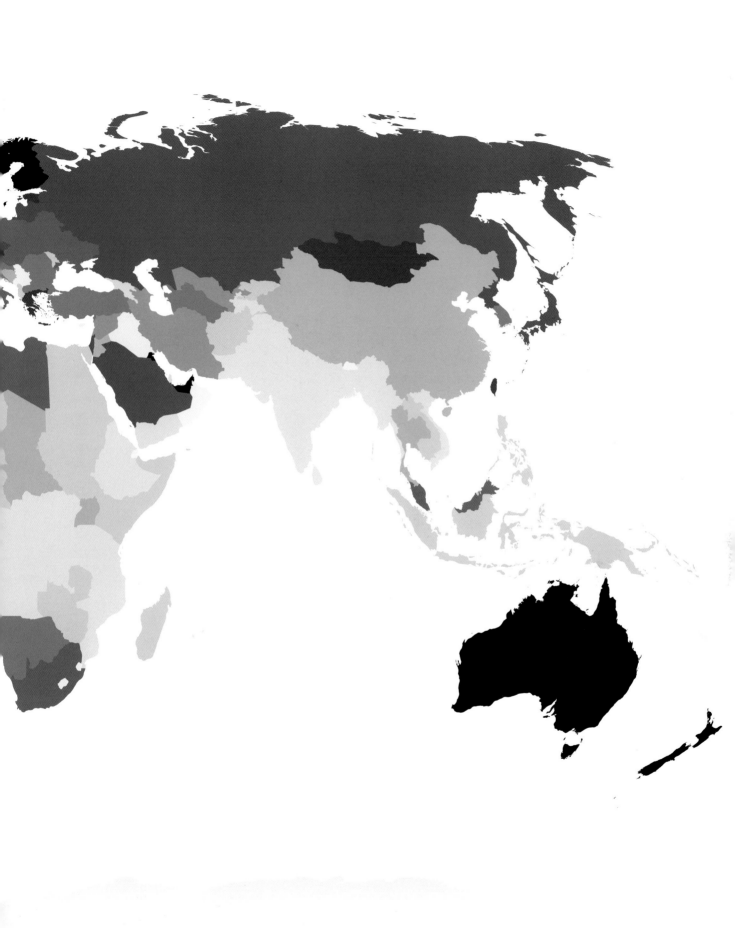

ECOLOGICAL FOOTPRINT PER CAPITA

The ecological footprint per capita measures the natural resources consumed by a nation divided by its population. This is the kind of map that shows us how unequal the world is and that the West is eating, burning and buying its way through the planet's resources at a rate that far exceeds any other part of the world. A small exception is found on the Arabian Peninsula, where, in the richest countries, the footprint is now comparable to North America or Europe.

Gabby Henrie, a map specialist who works at Pacific Cartography, first devised this map, and her figures point to a median figure for the ecological footprint per capita as 0.85. This means half the world's population have a footprint number above 0.85 and half below. The leap from 0.85 to the figure for the US, which comes in at 9.57, indicates a colossal rate of consumption in the US.

A wide range of resource use is assessed by determining footprint: from the power used to keep our washing machines chugging, to the water required to feed livestock. Nations that have big energy demands and high levels of consumerism come out worst, and poorer countries come out best. It is logical, too, to conclude that the West bears the heaviest responsibility for the problems that have accompanied industrialisation, including climate change, and should pick up the cost of fixing them. Although there is no one agreed way of measuring human footprint, and a particular country's place in the rankings varies between different approaches, they consistently show the West's culpability.

In the league table, the heaviest footprint belongs to the US, followed by the United Arab Emirates (8.97), Canada (8.56), Norway (8.17) and New Zealand (8.01). One explanation for these small countries taking the high slots is that they consume a lot of energy either heating or cooling their indoor environments.

Although these figures are per person (per capita), they reflect the society one lives in rather than personal habits. This means the figures are hard to shift. For example, the nature of the power and transport infrastructure in the US necessitates that even the most frugal community or individual will still use up more of the planet's resources than the average person in a far less developed country.

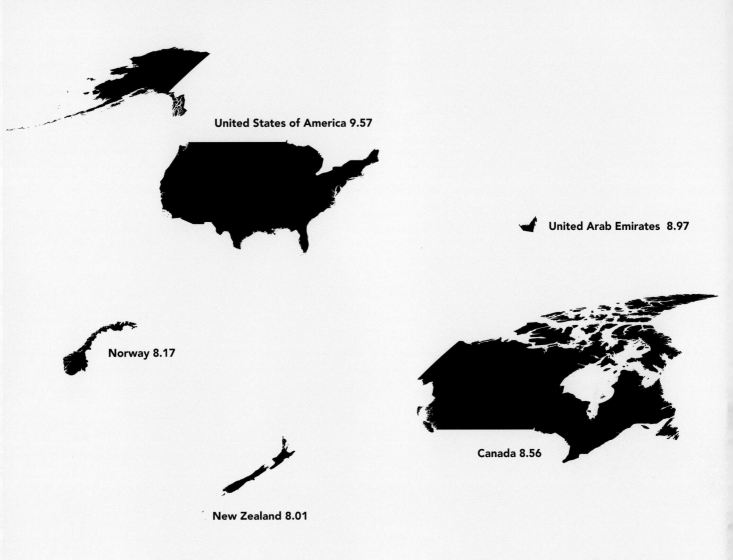

United States of America 9.57

United Arab Emirates 8.97

Norway 8.17

Canada 8.56

New Zealand 8.01

Five countries with the heaviest ecological footprint.

The link to development also means that as countries get wealthier, their footprint increases. We are already seeing this impact; it is apparent on the map in the darker shades creeping over Latin America and across East and South East Asia.

PEACEFULNESS

■ Least peaceful

■ Less peaceful

■ Average peace

■ Peaceful

■ Most peaceful

■ No data

PEACEFULNESS

A contiguous block of nations, stretching through Africa, the Middle East, Russia and South Asia, is plagued by violence and insecurity. Two of the standout features of the map, which is derived from 2015 data, are that, by and large, South America does not deserve the violent reputation it is so often given in films and news coverage, and that there is a rarely praised group of Southern African countries with levels of peacefulness that are comparable to those in Western Europe.

The map is based on the Global Peace Index (GPI), which is published by the Institute for Economics and Peace. The GPI is a composite of twenty-three indicators combined into one overall score. These indicators range across three main areas. First, ongoing domestic and international conflict; that is, the extent to which countries are involved in internal and external conflicts. Second, the level of discord within a nation. This includes factors such as crime rate, terrorist activity, violent demonstrations, an unstable political scene and the number of people forced to flee as refugees. The third area concerns militarisation, which includes factors such as military expenditure as a percentage of GDP and the number of armed service personnel per head.

The headline news is that a sharp split is emerging. Comparing this data with previous years, the Institute concludes that countries which were violent are getting much more so, while those that were peaceful are, by and large, staying that way. Thus the gap between the most and least peaceful countries is widening. Although the Institute tells us that there has been a decrease in military spending across the world, it warns that insurgency in the Middle East and North Africa points towards the 'internationalisation of modern conflict', and that countries 'thousands of kilometres away are affected by refugee flows or terrorism stemming from these conflicts'.

The two biggest factors giving countries bad GPI scores are terrorism and political instability. The Institute notes that only sixty-nine countries did not record a terrorist incident and that the intensity of terrorism is increasing, 'with

1. Iceland

1.192

2. Denmark

1.246

3. Austria

1.278

4. New Zealand

1.287

5. Portugal

1.356

Top five most peaceful countries with their Global Peace Index scores.

the number of countries suffering more than 500 deaths from terrorist acts more than doubling, up from 5 to 11'. The Institute also flags up the huge economic cost of violence, which it puts at almost $14 trillion, adding that 'the economic losses from conflict dwarf the expenditures and investments in peace-building and peacekeeping'. Perhaps more unexpectedly, it also notes that the number of armed service personnel fell in 48 of the 51 countries that it classifies as authoritarian. This drop appears to be due to the rise of more technologically driven militaries.

Since this map is drawn from country-specific data, we can name the best and worst performers. The most peaceful country in the world is Iceland, followed by Denmark, Austria, New Zealand and Portugal. The top 40 also include Bhutan, Singapore, Costa Rica, Qatar, Madagascar and, coming in at number 40, Zambia. The UK is 47 and the US falls much further down the list at 103 (below both Jamaica and Papua New Guinea). At the bottom of the list we find countries where a lack of peacefulness is endemic. Some will come as no surprise: Iraq, South Sudan and Syria take the last three slots. But the bottom 30 also include India, Turkey, Israel and Mexico.

THE BLACK MARBLE

THE BLACK MARBLE

The Black Marble, the earth at night, offers a vision of a sleeping world. Around the thin, twinkling patches of urban civilisation loom tracts of inky nothingness, echoing the white blanks of terra incognita that have swathed much older maps. Not that all of those lights represent throngs of humanity. There are great blobs of radiance where gas and oil flare into the night: in the middle of Australia and the least populated areas of North Africa, the Middle East and Russia.

And many urban areas are notable only for their absence of light. There is a sharp divide between South Korea and North Korea: the South shines brilliantly, but its kin to the north – at least beyond the tiny speck of the capital Pyongyang – is deep black. The bright lights of communism don't seem to be plugged in here. The geopolitics of illumination is one of the less explored but equally fascinating byways of the world map. If this portrait of the night-time planet had been captured a couple of decades ago, when Saddam Hussein ruled Iraq, they would have shown how he pooled that nation's electricity into two bright spots: Baghdad and his home town of Tikrit.

Lenin defined communism as 'Soviet government plus electrification', and light remains the prize and proof of progress; its absence compelling evidence of a failed or failing state. The bright spots of this map – Europe, the US, South and East Asia – are regions with a working infrastructure, where street lamps usually come on at night; where people have got used to flicking a switch and something happening.

Aside from patches at its edges, and the sinuous, shining valley of the Nile, this cannot be said for much of Africa, where heavily populated cities and towns are without reliable power supplies. One would think from this map that there were no people – and certainly no cities – in the Horn of Africa or Central Africa. But there are tens of millions of people; they just can't rely on a night-time power supply.

It's strangely comforting to imagine that everyone on the planet lays down their tired head and whispers good night to their fellow creatures at one and the same time. But of course the world does not have the same bedtime. What we see

A close-up look shows the high level of night-time activity that takes place along the Nile and in the small Gulf states.

here is a composite map assembled over nine days in April and 13 days in October 2012. During that time the Visible Infrared Imaging Radiometer Suite on board a NASA satellite captured the planet in vertical strips from pole to pole, making 312 orbits. It's not a one-off but an ongoing process; night light is now able to be continuously captured, and with a resolution that allows us to pick out individual fishing boats as well as the spread of wildfires and volcanic eruptions. The same imaging equipment shows up both the great loops of light from the Auroras that curl around the poles, and the bioluminescence of innumerable tiny sea creatures which causes swathes of the oceans to glow. The luminous world is not just a human creation.

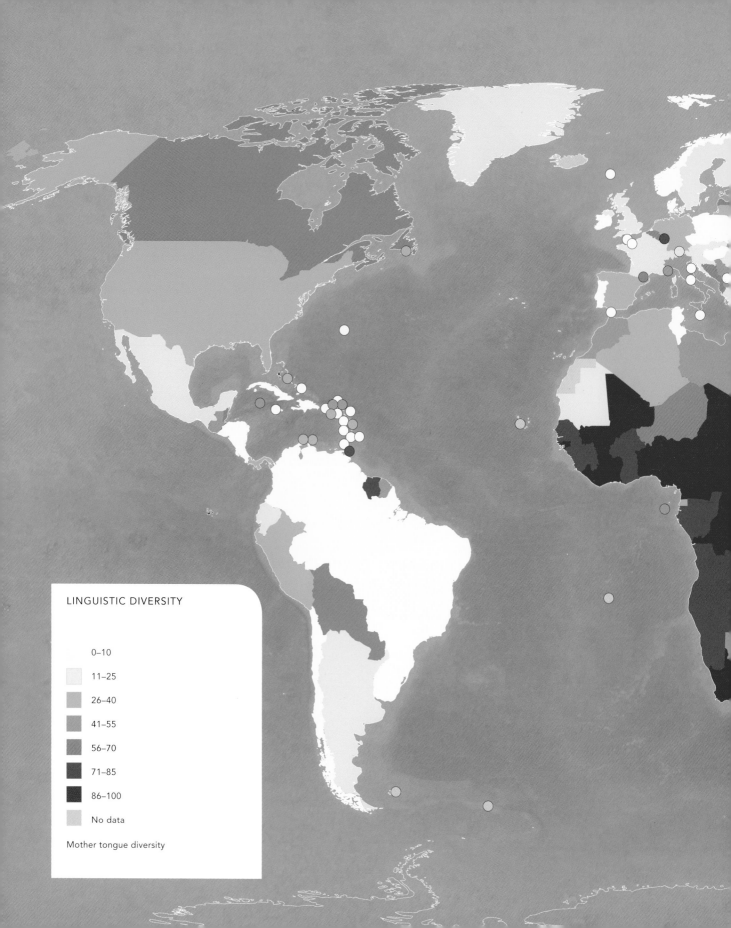

LINGUISTIC DIVERSITY

0–10

11–25

26–40

41–55

56–70

71–85

86–100

No data

Mother tongue diversity

One way of assessing a nation's linguistic diversity is by looking at the probability that two people selected at random from the population will have different mother tongues. It's an approach devised by the linguist Joseph Greenberg, and it's what this map is all about. In this version the index ranges from 0 (everyone has the same mother tongue) to 100 (no two people have the same mother tongue). The small dots represent distinct but tiny territories, such as Gibraltar.

The country with the highest score – the most linguistically diverse – is Papua New Guinea. Other regions whose diversity stands out are Sub-Saharan Africa, India and much of South East Asia. Countries with very low or zero scores include North and South Korea, Haiti and Cuba. Indeed, the lack of diversity across South and Central America is stark. There are plenty of languages in this part of the world, but not many people speak them. The same can be said for countries in regions with very diverse immigration patterns, such as North America and Western Europe. That's why these countries score low, while India, which has lots of languages and lots of people speaking them, scores high.

The map is derived from the 2015 edition of *Ethnologue*, a key reference work that contains statistics for thousands of languages.

It is worth returning to India in order to grasp just how wide diversity can be. India has about the same number of people as the entire continent of Africa. It also has about 1,700 languages and, more to the point, 30 of them are used by more than a million speakers per language. It's the size of those groups that means people are very likely to have to interact with others with a different mother tongue. Much the biggest group are the Hindi speakers, at over 400 million, but Tamil, Marathi, Telugu and Bengali each have 60 million speakers or more.

These kinds of numbers mean that being multilingual is something of a necessity for many Indians, who are often able to communicate in four or more languages. It also means that having English as a lingua franca can be very useful. Other English speakers find that status useful too: is has been estimated that 75 per cent of Americans and a whopping 95 per cent of Britons are monolingual.

**95% of Britons are
monolingual**

**Papua New Guinea is
the most linguistically
diverse**

**75% of Americans
are monolingual**

When it comes to enumerating languages, a word of caution is in order. As soon as you think you've identified one, someone will tell you that it has a variety of dialects, some of which can be classified as separate languages. Many people see Italy as a country with, apart from some German, French and Ladin in the north, one mother tongue – Italian. But others argue that Italy has numerous regional languages, from Sardinian to Friulian. And what's true of Italy is just as true for India or any of the other shaded areas of the map. How languages get defined and counted is rarely straightforward or uncontroversial.

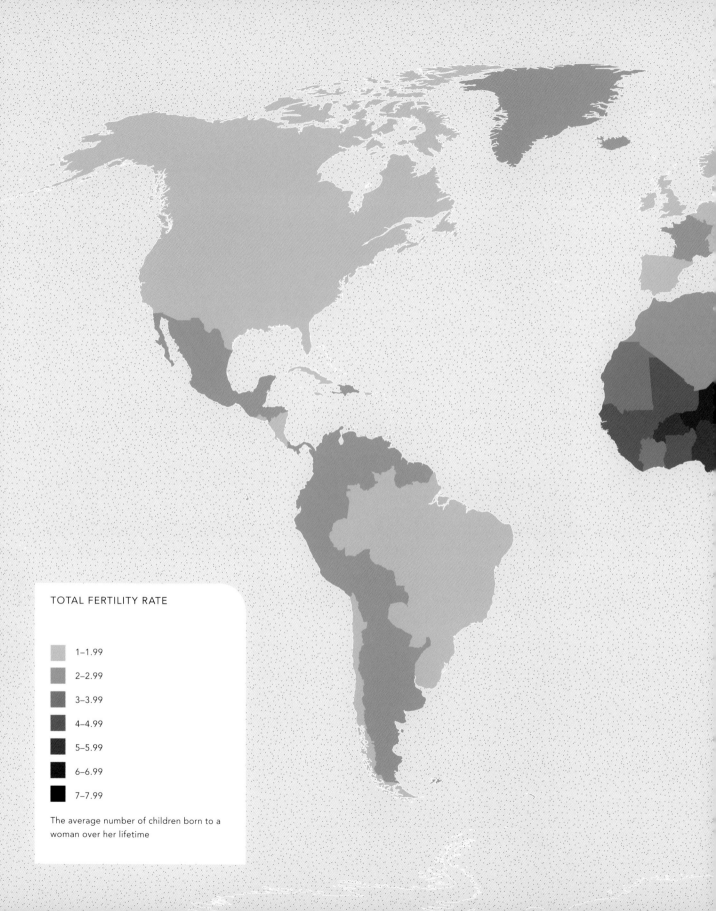

TOTAL FERTILITY RATE

1–1.99

2–2.99

3–3.99

4–4.99

5–5.99

6–6.99

7–7.99

The average number of children born to a
woman over her lifetime

TOTAL FERTILITY RATE

The old view of global fertility rates was that they were low in the developed north and high in the so-called 'Third World'. But now we see Africa standing out against a sea of much lighter hues, surrounded by areas where women have far fewer children. Africa has become the exception, with family sizes well above those found in Asia and Latin America. The fact that Africa contains so many of the least developed, poorest and least educated countries of the world provides the clearest explanation of this situation. While other nations, such as India and Brazil, have grown wealthy enough to transition to smaller families, this has yet to occur in most parts of Africa. We can see, though, that there is a significant difference between South Africa and Botswana in the south, Morocco, Algeria, Libya and Tunisia in the north and the rest of the continent, where fertility rates remain markedly high.

At the centre of any explanation of fertility rates is the position of women in society. Given the choice, women rarely choose to have so many children. It not only interferes with their economic independence and access to education, it is dangerous, and Sub-Saharan Africa has the highest maternal death rate in the world (about 1,000 maternal deaths per 100,000 live births). By 2050, Nigeria's population is projected to be nearly the same size as the US, and by the end of the century, if current trends persist, it will be over 750,000,000.

Forecasts predict that, by 2050, one out of every three children born in the world will be African. However, fears of overpopulation should be tempered by the probability that African states will begin to take the same path seen elsewhere, and fertility rates will decline. It is also worth remembering that the total population of Africa is about the same as India's. At the moment it is one of the least populous parts of the world, and for those interested in overpopulation, it is better to look at places such as Europe, which are much more crowded.

In other ways this map, which is drawn from 2015 data, tells a positive story. It shows that for the majority of the world, status and educational attainment for women has improved along with access to contraception. The majority of

What the total fertility rate might look like in 2070. This UN forecast shows declines everywhere but the contrast between rates in Africa and the rest of the world growing even greater.

countries have policies encouraging family planning and access to contraception. Some policies have gone to greater extremes, such as China's one-child policy, which ended in 2016, and sterilisation campaigns in India. However, the two biggest factors in creating smaller family size are economic growth and the empowerment of women.

The total fertility rate is not the same as the birth rate. Birth rate is the yearly number of births per thousand of population and is a rather crude snapshot. Total fertility rate takes a longer view, although it is a more complex calculation. It is the average number of children that would be born per woman if all of the women in the population lived to the end of their childbearing years and bore children according to the age-specific fertility rates for that country and period. Without immigration, population size declines when the total fertility rate is lower than 2.1 children per female.

RELIGIOUS DIVERSITY

Low

Moderate

High

Very high

RELIGIOUS DIVERSITY

Prepare to be surprised: it seems that the world's largest communist country is also one of its most religiously diverse. And that there is a world arc of diversity that takes in most of the north of the planet as well as East and South Asia. The picture in Africa is highly uneven, with diverse societies sitting next to homogeneous ones, while Central and South America is, pretty much, a large block of religious uniformity.

Religious diversity can be measured in many ways. This map, which is based on 2010 data, looks at the percentage of each country's population that belongs to eight major religious groups. The closer a country comes to having equal shares of the eight groups, the higher its rating. It's not a map of religious tolerance; it doesn't tell us anything about how diversity is viewed or accepted. Neither does it delve into religious subgroups. The Center for the Study of Global Christianity estimated that in 2012 there were 43,000 Christian denominations – if that sort of data was taken into consideration, the map would look rather different.

Understanding the nature of the eight groups makes the map a bit less surprising. Five are pretty obvious – Buddhism, Christianity, Hinduism, Islam and Judaism – the 'big five', each of which originated in either the Middle East or India and which now account for roughly three-quarters of the world's population. The other three are more interesting, in the sense that they are less widely recognised. One of the groups covers the religiously unaffiliated, and this includes atheists and agnostics. This may come as a revelation, since such people are not usually thought of as religious, but, on reflection, it is sensible: doubters and non-believers have a clear religious viewpoint and are still part of the spectrum and diversity of religious belief. Societies where atheism is outlawed or considered outlandish can never be classified as truly diverse, but societies where it is prevalent, such as China, may be. The remaining two groups comprise adherents of minority religions. This includes so-called tribal and folk religions as well as small yet still widely practised religions such as Baha'i, Jainism, Shintoism, Sikhism, Taoism, Tenrikyo, Wicca and Zoroastrianism.

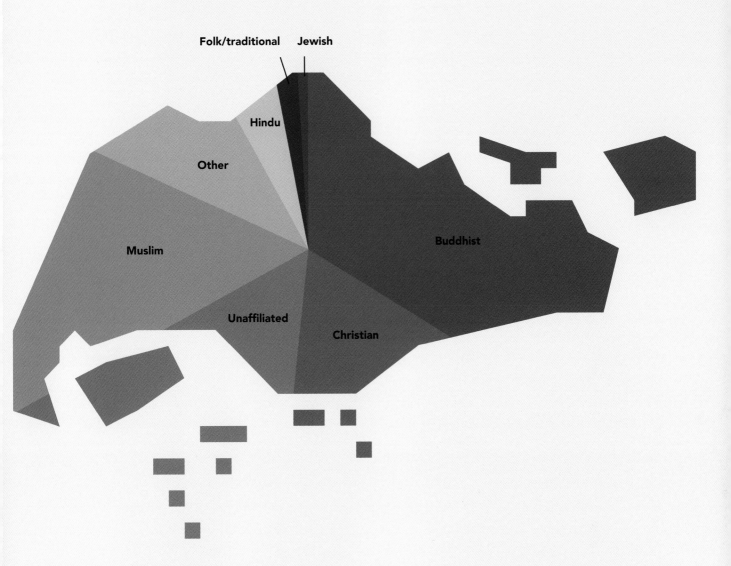

Folk/traditional   **Jewish**

Hindu

Other

Muslim

Buddhist

Unaffiliated

Christian

The most religiously diverse country is Singapore. This graphic shows the size of different beliefs represented on a stylised national map.

The Pew Research Center, which came up with this eightfold categorisation system and collected the data this map is derived from, arrived at the conclusion that out of all the countries it looked at, Singapore was the most religiously diverse. About a third of Singapore's population is Buddhist, 18 per cent are Christian, 16 per cent are religiously unaffiliated, 14 per cent are Muslim, 10 per cent belong to 'other religions', 5 per cent are Hindu, 2 per cent belong to folk or traditional religions and fewer than one per cent are Jewish. The bottom nine countries – the least diverse in the world – are an interesting mix: Papua New Guinea, Western Sahara, Iran, Romania, Tunisia, Timor-Leste, Afghanistan, Somalia and, coming in joint last place, Tokelau, Morocco and Vatican City.

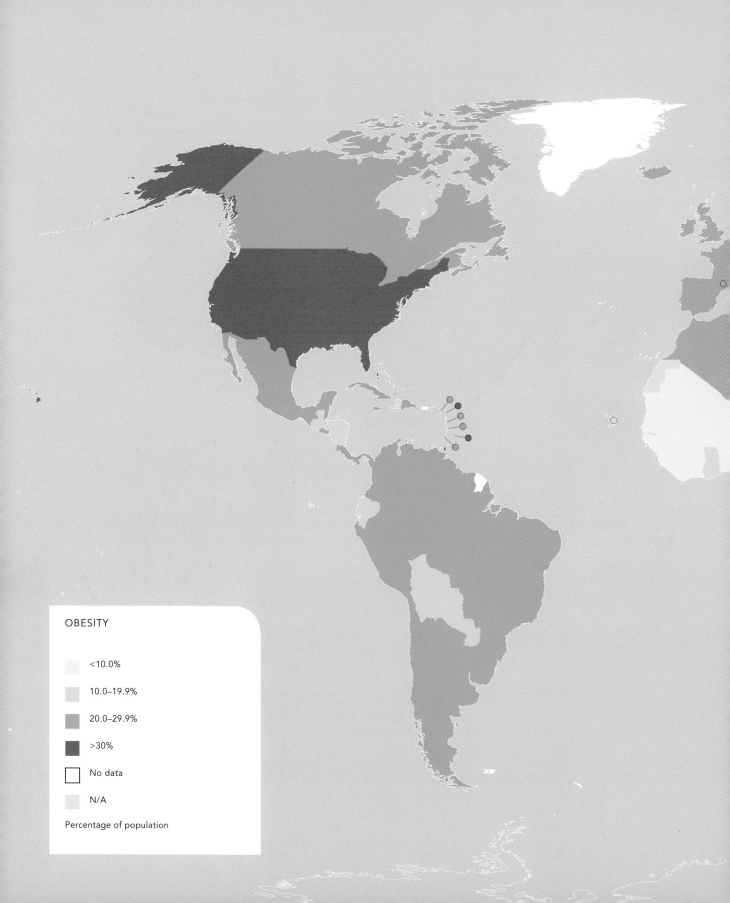

OBESITY

- <10.0%
- 10.0–19.9%
- 20.0–29.9%
- >30%
- No data
- N/A

Percentage of population

OBESITY

More than half a billion people worldwide are obese. It's a global issue, and one of the biggest health challenges we face. It's also an issue in which maps can help us get a handle on which parts of the world face the greatest challenges.

This map draws on World Health Organisation (WHO) data from 2014, and shows that the prevalence of obesity is highest in the Americas (27 per cent) and lowest in South East Asia (5 per cent). To be 'obese' means that you have a BMI of over 30 kg/m^2. BMI stands for body mass index, and it is arrived at by dividing your weight by the square of your height. It will come as no surprise that the US contains the highest proportion of people who are obese. However, it is less well known that people in the Middle East are just as likely to be obese as people in Europe and the Americas, particularly in Saudi Arabia and Libya.

The most marked separation between countries with an obesity issue and countries where it is rare is that which divides North Africa and the countries of Sub-Saharan Africa. The WHO's commentary on this map states that 'the prevalence of raised body mass index increases with the income level', and that 'the overall prevalence' of obesity is 'over four times higher in high-income countries compared to low-income countries'. This might be a useful fact, but the map shows us that, as an explanation, it is a sweeping generalisation. The countries of East Asia, including Japan, have relatively high income levels, but here obesity is rare. Indeed, the difference in rates between the US and Canada, and the equivalence of rates between relatively poor countries in Europe and richer ones, suggests that income is not a sufficient explanation. Another key cause is dietary differences. Indeed, the dark colours on the map all point to cultures where meat and dairy products are a daily expectation. The light colours in East Asia reflect dietary cultures with more fish and less of a reliance on diary.

Looking more closely, some other patterns are revealed. Those nations with the worst obesity problem are in neither the Americas nor North Africa, but in the Pacific. The Pacific Island nations such as American Samoa, Samoa and Tonga regularly top the rankings as the places on the planet where obesity is most

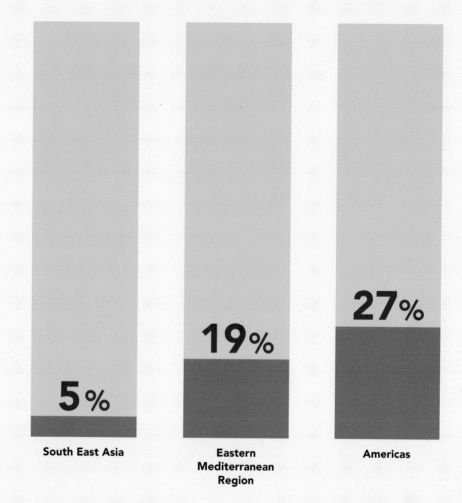

● Obese

South East Asia

Eastern Mediterranean Region

Americas

widespread. The shift in diet towards meat and dairy, a sedentary lifestyle and a culture that still associates big bodies with status and wealth all appear to be responsible.

But perhaps the geographical variability shown on this map is less important than its index. With the darker colours indicating the presence of over 20 per cent obesity in the population, it shows us that being overweight is a major issue and one that is common across much of the world. Although there are countervailing trends in richer countries, where people in the upper-income bracket often prefer and can afford a healthy diet, a key driver of our overeating planet is that rising incomes are not translating into a diet of sushi and skinny lattes, but instead are offering access to plentiful, highly processed and fattening foods.

HAPPINESS

- ■ 2.86–3.80
- ■ 3.81–4.75
- ■ 4.76–5.70
- ■ 5.71–6.65
- ■ 6.66–7.60
- ☐ No data

Self-assessed scores, where 0 equals worst
possible life and 10 the best

HAPPINESS

Money may not buy you love but it looks like it buys you happiness. This map shows self-reported happiness by country. It's immediately apparent that the world's poorest places, in Africa and much of the Middle East and South Asia, are not as happy as elsewhere. The rich states of the Arabian Peninsula stand out as contented and much of the Western world is in the same position. One apparent counter to this thesis is Latin America. It seems that at least some people there are just as happy as the wealthier folk north of the Rio Grande. This is a bit of a head-scratcher; though it's worth noting that GDP per capita across Latin America is similar to Russia's.

This map is derived from the *World Happiness Report* published in 2015. The first *World Happiness Report* came out in 2012, a product of the 'United Nations High Level Meeting on Happiness and Well-Being' which followed a plea by the Prime Minister of Bhutan for countries to start taking happiness seriously. Some have heeded the call: the National Agenda of the United Arab Emirates sets out a goal 'to be the happiest of all nations'.

What is being measured here is feelings of wellbeing. The different shades on our map show averages for the period 2012–2014 and are based on polling in which people were asked to evaluate the quality of their current lives on a scale of 0 to 10, where 0 represents the worst possible life and 10 the best. The *World Happiness Report* breaks down this data to show how particular factors influence happiness. It turns out that GDP per capita is just one of the determinants; other key influences are social support, healthy life expectancy, freedom to make life choices, generosity and freedom from corruption. Income clearly matters but it's not the end of the story: being part of a caring, healthy and open society is also important.

The list of the most and least happy nations of the 158 surveyed has some predictable as well as some surprising entrants. At the top is Switzerland followed by Iceland, Denmark, Norway, Canada, Finland, Netherlands, Sweden, New Zealand and Australia. The USA comes in at 15, one below Mexico and one above

1. Norway

2. Denmark

3. Iceland

4. Switzerland

5. Finland

Northern Europe is still the happiest part of the world according to the 2017 *World Happiness Report*.

Brazil. The UK is 21, one below the United Arab Emirates but above Germany (26), France (29), Spain (36) and Italy (50). My unscientific and entirely flippant theory of why people in the famously moan-prone UK appear to be happier than many of their European neighbours is that they enjoy complaining: being grumpy is their way of having fun. The opposite end of the table is largely made up of African states. The only non-African countries in the bottom ten are Syria and Afghanistan.

GLOBALISATION

TWITTER RELATIONSHIPS

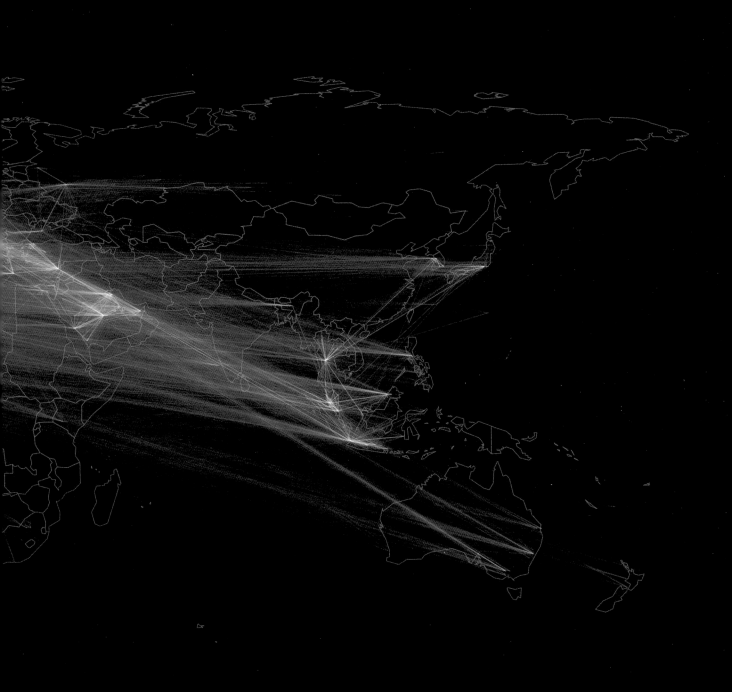

Despite being limited to 140 characters, Twitter messages have become a barometer of world opinion. This map looks at a particular species of tweet: the retweet, in which users forward a tweet to which they want to draw attention. Seen in this way, it is a map showing which parts of the world are interested in each other and which aren't – at least in the Twittersphere – and it's distilled from all the retweets sent between 23 October 2012 and 30 November 2012.

After much collating and sieving of the data, the final image is of the strongest 42,000 connections. Many of the patterns are clear: there are big sweeps of light across the Atlantic and down through the Arabian Peninsula to the cities of South East Asia. Conversely, North and South America aren't as interested in each other as one might expect. Europe and South America have a much stronger retweeting bond. Twitter is banned in China, so it's no surprise the connections in East Asia skip over China's great cities and go straight to South Korea and Japan.

This image was put together by a team of information scientists at the University of Illinois at Urbana-Champaign. It is a thing of beauty. The lines of light leap across the world stage with balletic grace. The eye is naturally drawn by the longest lines; the ones that connect the continents. But on closer inspection it becomes apparent that most retweets are much more local. The East Coast of the US is the busiest hub both in that country and on the planet, and across the world people are more likely to retweet messages from nearer than from further away. Apparently users who retweet or reference another user just the once have an average distance between them of around 800 miles (over 1,000km), but that distance plummets as the number of those retweets increases.

Even after simplifying all the lines of connection, the density of messaging in some parts of the world is startling. Of the world's 328 million active Twitter users at the start of 2017, 70 million live in the US and about 14 million in the UK. As the maps suggests, the numbers in Africa are much lower, with about 2 million users in Nigeria, the continent's most populous country. If, as Twitter insists, it is

United Kingdom

14

million users

United States of America

70

million users

Nigeria

2

million users

The approximate number of active Twitter users in three countries out of a global total of 328 million (2017 first quarter).

'the pulse of the planet', then our planetary heartbeat is much stronger in some places than in others.

The Illinois team compared Twitter coverage with mainstream media and found that the latter has 'significantly less coverage of Latin America and vastly greater of Africa' and that, overall, 'mainstream media appears to have more even coverage' of our world than Twitter.

The Illinois team compiled a whole series of Twitter maps to give us a comprehensive view of its practices, habits and geography. They have arrived at some fascinating insights. In most parts of the world, they tell us, users stick to their own language in their Twitter message but offer their location in English. So the location field is filled in with such expressions as 'Paris – the City of Light!' or 'Tokyo, my home of homes'. They suggest one possible explanation is that this 'represents an attempt by users across the world to ensure that their tweets at least appear in search results', and that although users 'don't care that English speakers know what they are saying', nevertheless 'they do want them to know they exist.'

US FAST-FOOD FRANCHISES

- None
- <10
- 10–50
- 50–100
- 100–200
- >200

Number of outlets per million people

The spread of US fast-food franchises is not just about the spread of fast food – it is also about the success of the franchise model for doing business. It is a model that allows a company to pass on risk to the franchise owners, who, in turn, benefit from being able to buy their own slice of an up-and-running and successful retail brand. This map shows us fast-food outlets per million people, and is based on the numbers of five franchise operations: McDonald's, Subway, Pizza Hut, Starbucks and KFC.

Every country has its own version of fast food. In any city in the world you'll find street vendors selling everything from deep-fried falafels to bowls of noodles. It's fast and it's cheap. What it isn't is American fast food, which is a standardised product delivered in an instantly recognisable environment. The map shows us that there are some parts of the world which have developed quite a taste for it. Australia and the UK are keen, but so too is Iceland, the United Arab Emirates and Malaysia.

Conversely, there is a big chunk of Africa where you can't get a McDonald's for love nor money. It would be wishful thinking to imagine that this is because people have rejected US fast food in favour of traditional fare. A more likely explanation is that economic development has not yet reached the level required to create enough entrepreneurs or customers wealthy enough to make these outlets viable.

The different franchises are not spread evenly across the world. McDonald's is the big player in Europe, but KFC is more successful in East and South East Asia. In 2013, the number of KFCs in China outstripped the number in the US. The fact that China isn't glowing brightly on this map reflects its large population rather than the scarcity of US fast food. Subway has been one of the more recent success stories, expanding rapidly in Europe, Asia and the Americas. It now has some 45,000 restaurants in 112 countries (McDonald's has about 36,500 restaurants).

Not all US fast-food companies have turned themselves into global players, and some, like White Castle, tried but failed. Many others, from Taco Bell to Krispy Kreme Doughnuts, are forging ahead. And, despite periodic reports about

McDonalds's

36,500 restaurants in

119

countries

KFC

19,955 restaurants in

123

countries

Starbucks

20,995 outlets in

70

countries

Subway

44,810 restaurants in

112

countries

Pizza Hut

16,125 restaurants in

59

countries

A snapshot of worldwide food empires. Subway has expanded to become one of the biggest global fast food providers.

the declining fortunes of individual companies, the world still seems to have an appetite for US fast food. At the moment the US is unique; other countries have developed their own fast-food franchises but they haven't spread beyond their own shores. In what is supposed to be a competitive marketplace, it is a little curious: when it comes to international fast food, the choice is between the American model or nothing.

SHIPPING ROUTES

Vessel routes

SHIPPING ROUTES

In a world where the Internet and air travel appear to be dominant, it is useful to be reminded that most of the things we import and export are transported by ship. Many argue that, in the words of *The Economist*, the container ship 'has been more of a driver of globalisation than all trade agreements in the past 50 years taken together'. Container ships have transformed what was once a labour-intensive, costly and unwieldy activity into an automated and cost-effective global system.

About 60 per cent of shipped trade is transported in containers, and the rest in the holds of bulk freighters. The ships plotted on our map are trying to find the 'great-circle distance', which is the shortest distance between two points on the surface of a sphere. It's not an easy thing to find on a planet that has so much land in the way. The routes that stand out most strongly are the much-travelled lanes across the North Pacific and North Atlantic, as well as those that run from East and South Asia across the Indian Ocean and up to Europe, either through Egypt's Suez Canal or round South Africa's Cape of Good Hope.

Two other key pinch points are the Straits of Malacca, a narrow waterway between the Malay Peninsula and Sumatra, and the Strait of Hormuz, through which any ship entering the Persian Gulf must pass.

In the Americas, the bunching of tracks around Central America is created by the large number of vessels headed for the Panama Canal. The fact that so many ships are still choosing to take the long route around South America and Africa reflects a problem with the world's shipping canals: they aren't big enough for the new generation of super-sized ships. The 'Panamax' and 'Suezmax' specifications tell captains whether their vessel will make it through. The first 'post-Panamax' ship – a ship too big for the Panama Canal – was the RMS *Queen Mary*, launched in 1934. In the 1980s a new generation of post-Panamax leviathans set sail, creating a serious challenge for this global gateway. Far bigger locks were built and opened in 2016, but the largest container ships still can't squeeze through and have to go the long way round.

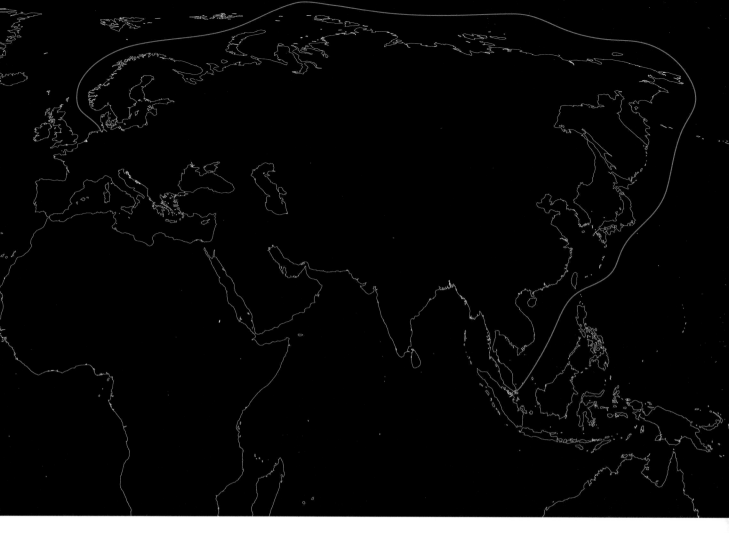

As the Arctic ice melts, new routes are opening, such as the Northern Sea Route between Singapore and Germany.

'Chinamax' is another new nautical term. It's a standard measure of fully laden ship size, but it's also a word that tells us where much of the world's shipping is now coming from. Shipping trade is often measured in terms of a ship's cargo-carrying capacity with a unit called the Twenty-Foot Equivalent Unit (TEU). The world's biggest route is Asia–North America, which at over 23,000,000 TEU dwarfs the next biggest route, which is Asia–Northern Europe at 13,700,000 TEU.

The direction of trade is, perhaps, even more telling. On the Asia–North America route, more than twice as much cargo is heading east towards North America than is going in the other direction. Similarly, on the Asia–Northern Europe route, over 9,000,000 TEU is going towards Northern Europe, but only 4,500,000 TEU are going from Northern Europe to Asia.

All those lines stretched across the map also tell us about where things are being made and where they are being consumed.

ENERGY FLUX

— Pipelines

— Transmission lines

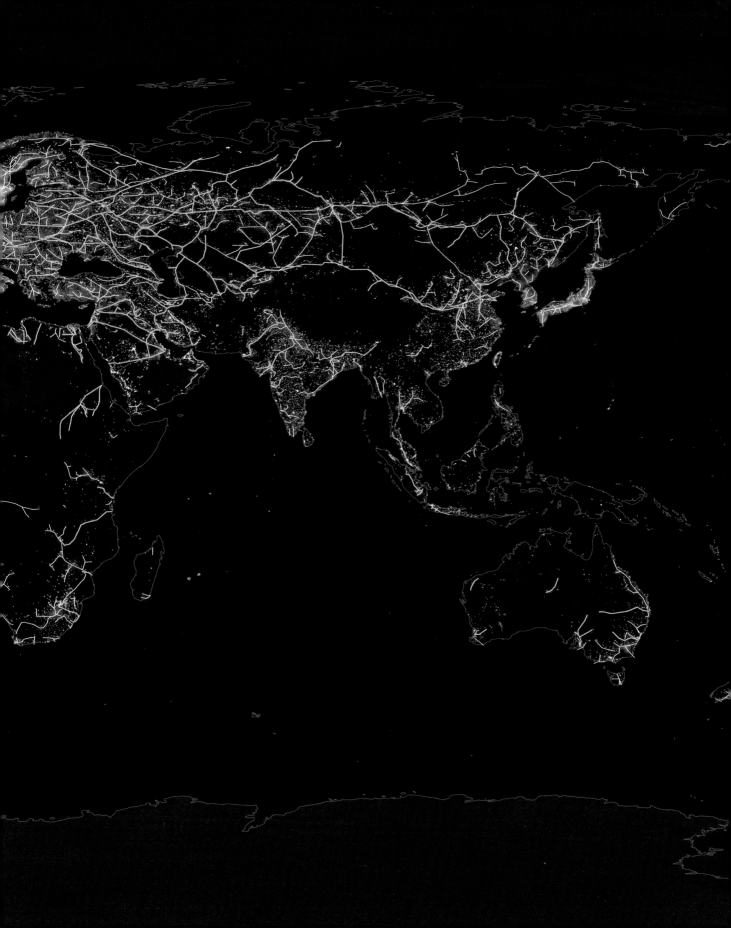

ENERGY FLUX

It has been estimated that the world has spent $100 trillion over the last 100 years in creating an energy infrastructure. We can see the result on this map, and where the money has gone. The electricity transmission in white and the pipelines carrying mainly oil and gas in yellow are densely packed across a brightly lit and sprawling area of Europe which sends tendrils to feed deep into the surrounding regions. Long yellow pipelines suck hydrocarbons from far away in the oilfields of Siberia and the Middle East. The US and the southern rim of Canada provide another intense region of activity, as do East Asia and Japan. India stands out, too, because of its comprehensive electricity infrastructure.

Most of the dark regions of the map tell us that there are not many people living there. It is worth recalling that India's population is about the same as the entire continent of Africa, so it's no surprise that that great continent isn't covered with pipelines. However, populous African areas, such as the West African coast, are clearly under-connected. Much of Nigeria would be glowing as brightly as Europe if people there had access to energy in the way Europeans do. Some totally dark areas register a catastrophic breakdown of supply.

This image is derived from the work of Globaïa, a Canadian non-profit organisation that has issued a series of maps under the title *Cartography of the Anthropocene*. The Anthropocene is a new era in geological time which has come about from human impacts to the earth. Some geologists dislike the term, and consider it a kind of conceit to imagine that we're so important as a species, but others concede that we have fundamentally altered the environment, in large part as a consequence of the kind of infrastructure mapped here.

Seen from afar, the transmission of energy looks like one vast interconnected whole. But it isn't. As those long yellow lines indicate, provided you install some pumping stations, there are no limits to the lengths of gas or oil pipelines that can be laid. It's different for electricity. The crackling noise you hear near transmission cables is lost electricity; and the sag in the wires is partly because they're hot and so have expanded – another sign of power loss. This leaky system explains why

Map showing the full combination of human systems: transportation, communication networks and energy infrastructures across the world.

the white lines on the map are much shorter than the yellow. It presents a perennial challenge to engineers, which, if it could be cracked, would mean a revolution for the world's power supply. Recently it has been found that superconductors in super-cold temperatures can bring us electricity in underground cables with virtually no power loss – but at very great expense. The hunt for efficient long-distance solutions continues.

NUMBER OF MIGRANTS

<2%

2–5%

5–10%

10–15%

15–20%

20–40%

>40%

Migrants as percentage of population,
2015 data

NUMBER OF MIGRANTS

There are some glaring divides in the size of the migrant population between different countries. The Middle East and Central Asia show some of the most drastic contrasts. The proportion of foreign migrants in Oman, Jordan and Israel was over 40 per cent in 2015 and, in Saudi Arabia, it was nearly as large, but next door in Yemen and Iraq, it remains tiny. In some ways this is a map of prosperity, safety and accessibility. No one wants to live in a country that is not safe. It's clear that people are finding those advantages in many countries in the West, but also in pockets of affluence elsewhere.

One of the large areas of blue on this map sits just below Russia: it's the Central Asian country of Kazakhstan. An oil-rich nation, it has over two million Russians, as well as a growing population of migrants from its other neighbours. Other interesting contrasts may be better known, such as the fact that Canada has a larger percentage of migrants than the US, and that Australia and New Zealand continue to be big draws.

In Africa, South America and South and East Asia there are huge swathes of low-migration countries. The notion that the whole world is now cosmopolitan, with people of all nations living everywhere, may have its appeal but it is a gross exaggeration. India, China and Japan may be diverse in many ways, but not many people from other nations live there. Perhaps the world is dividing up into countries where lots of migrants live and countries where they are pretty rare. There certainly seems to be a trend for those countries that attract other nationalities to attract even more, and there is, currently, little sign that much of Asia is becoming cosmopolitan in the way that so much of Western Europe and some of the Middle East has done.

The number of international migrants worldwide keeps growing. In 2000, there were 173 million international migrants; in 2015 that had risen to 244 million, a figure that includes 20 million refugees. This is a map of percentages, but in absolute terms nearly two-thirds of international migrants live in Europe (76 million) or Asia (75 million) with North America having the third-largest number

<100,000

Peru
Morocco
Mongolia
Nicaragua
Honduras
Guatemala
Namibia

76
Million
Europe

54
Million
North America

75
Million
Asia

Nearly two-thirds of international migrants live in Europe or Asia.

(54 million). Two-thirds of all international migrants live in just 20 countries, with the largest number in the US, followed by Germany, Russia and Saudi Arabia. Yet, as we have seen, the flip side of this concentration is that there are many countries with very few migrants, more evidence that suggests a division has grown between the cosmopolitan and non-cosmopolitan nations of the world.

NORTH AMERICA

LATIN AMERICA

OCEANIA

ASIA (SOUTH EAST)

ASIA (EAST)

ASIA (SOUTH)

MIDDLE EAST

NORTH AMERICA

■ United States

■ Canada

AFRICA

■ Morocco

■ Egypt

■ Côte d'Ivoire

■ Burkina Faso

■ Ghana

■ Nigeria

■ Zimbabwe

■ South Africa

EUROPE

■ United Kingdom

■ Germany

■ France

■ Netherlands

■ Switzerland

■ Spain

■ Italy

■ Portugal

RUSSIA AND CENTRAL ASIA

■ Ukraine

■ Russia

■ Kazakhstan

■ Uzbekistan

MIDDLE EAST

■ United Arab Emirates

■ Saudi Arabia

■ Qatar

■ Syria

■ Jordan

■ Kuwait

■ Bahrain

■ Israel

LATIN AMERICA

■ Mexico

■ Brazil

■ Peru

OCEANIA

■ New Zealand

■ Australia

ASIA (SOUTH EAST)

■ Vietnam

■ Thailand

■ Myanmar

■ Singapore

■ Indonesia

■ Philippines

■ Malaysia

ASIA (EAST)

■ Japan

■ Hong Kong

■ China

ASIA (SOUTH)

■ India

■ Afghanistan

■ Iran

■ Pakistan

Outer ring = destination country

Inner ring = origin country

EUROPE

RUSSIA AND CE

Chord diagrams are a new way of representing complex data, especially data that involves a plethora of connections. Although first used in 2007 to visualise information about genomes, these diagrams have proved popular with migration researchers. Like the maps in this book, they offer information in visual terms: they simplify, and don't offer fine detail, but what we do get is the big picture. Putting so much information about bilateral flows of migration onto a world map would look like a plate of spaghetti, but with a circular model it looks rather beautiful.

Knowing just three things – that each country has its own colour, that continents are grouped into broad colour bands (for example, the European countries are different shades of green) and that the chord colours represent country of origin – we can already start using the diagram. If we combine these three facts with just one more, that chord thickness represents the size of the flow of people, we are in an even better position.

We can see that Europe, on the right-hand side of the circle, is a receiver rather than a sender of people, and that much of its migration is coming from Africa and the Americas. Looking up to the top left, we can see a fat chunk of yellow going from Mexico to the US, indicating the scale of migration from the former to the latter. Turning to the purple loops within the purple rim on the right, it is clear that much of the migration in the former Soviet Union occurs within that region. Another pattern that can be picked out is the large flow of people from particular Asian countries, shown in blue, to the Gulf States.

There are just a couple of other features to note if we are to be an even more proficient user of the chord diagram. The very outer ring is coloured by destination countries for emigrants and the next ring in shows the origin country of immigrants. Some countries don't have much of an outer ring because they are mostly receiving migrants; conversely, other countries have a small inner ring because they are mostly sending migrants. There are very few countries where these two rings are of similar length, although if we look over to the African segment we will spot a few. Looking further into the origin and destination points

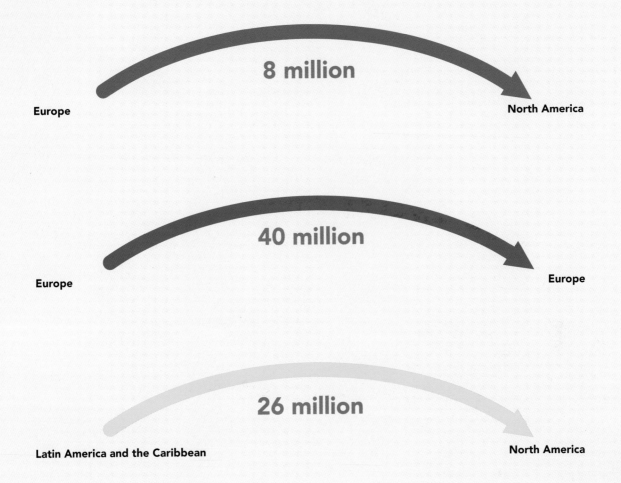

8 million

Europe   North America

40 million

Europe   Europe

26 million

Latin America and the Caribbean   North America

Origins and destinations of
international migrants up to 2015.

for these countries, it becomes apparent that there is a lot of internal migration within Africa, as well as considerable emigration from Africa.

This attractive diagram derives from the work of population specialists at the Vienna Institute of Demography and makes use of a software package that visualises data in circular form called Circos. The diagram is based on the number of people who changed country between 2005 and 2010, and more specifically an estimate for those 50 countries that sent or received at least 0.5 per cent of the world's migrants.

PEOPLE LIVING IN THE US
BORN OUTSIDE THE US

- <1,000
- 1–10k
- 10–90k
- 100–240k
- 250–490k
- 500–990k
- >1m

One in five international migrants live in the US. In 2015, 46,630,000 people living in the US were born in other countries. This map shows where they are from. The countries with the highest number of emigrants to the US are shown in dark purple. There is a huge disparity between the top slot in the group and the rest. Mexico is by far the largest origin point of migrants to the US, with a little over twelve million Mexicans making the journey north.

The US's immigrant population dwarfs that of Germany, the world's next largest migrant destination, which itself has about 12,000,000 immigrants. After Mexico, the largest group to the US is from China, with 2,100,000, followed by India (1,970,000), the Philippines (1,900,000), Puerto Rico (1,740,000), Vietnam (1,300,000), El Salvador (1,280,000), Cuba (1,130,000), South Korea (1,120,000) and the Dominican Republic (940,000).

A striking aspect of the list of people coming to the US is its diversity: this is a multicultural migration pattern, bringing people from South America, the Caribbean, South Asia, East and South East Asia. And although the numbers from the top 10 sending nations exceed all the other migrants put together, there is a long tail of countries with smaller but still significant flows of migration. Those countries shown in purple – the next category down from dark purple – tell us that there are large numbers of German- (630,000), British- (710,000) and, least surprisingly, Canadian-born (840,000) people living in the US.

There is no nation on earth that hasn't seen some scale of migration to the US. This could also be said of Canada and many countries in Western Europe, which have all seen migration patterns that are characterised by their size but also by their incredible variety. The great capitals of the West can justifiably boast that they are home to people from every corner of the world.

Interesting to note, too, is that the percentage of those who want to leave is very small. In 2015, only around one per cent of people born in the US lived outside of that nation, a far smaller figure than many other Western countries.

The diverse and distant countries that have the largest emigrant populations in the US.

The data for this map includes estimates of the number of unauthorised migrants and is derived from the Pew Research Center, a non-partisan US 'fact tank'. They point out that although the absolute numbers are large, they do not add up to an overwhelming percentage of the US population. About 14 per cent of people in the US are foreign-born, a much lower figure than Canada (22 per cent) or Australia (28 per cent). Interestingly, recent Pew Center research shows that more Mexicans are now leaving than arriving in the US.

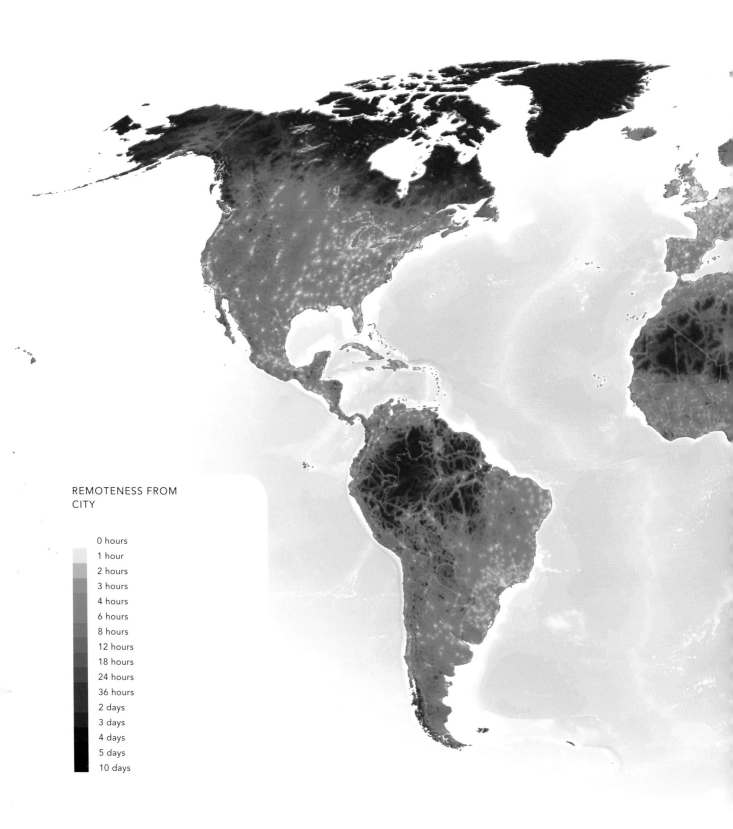

REMOTENESS FROM
CITY

0 hours
1 hour
2 hours
3 hours
4 hours
6 hours
8 hours
12 hours
18 hours
24 hours
36 hours
2 days
3 days
4 days
5 days
10 days

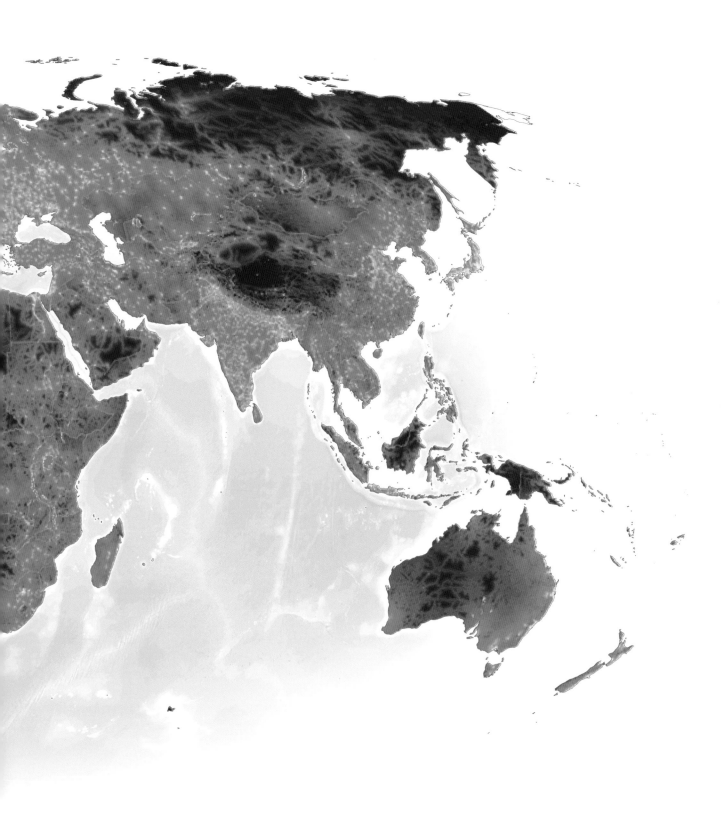

Our idea of remoteness is still bound to how far we live from the city. In the era of the Internet, one might expect this association to have weakened, but in reality there are multiple amenities that are not available in the deep countryside, from access to medical care to political and cultural events. The dark patches on this map represent seriously deep country: travel time to the city in these places has to be measured in days rather than hours, and the scale goes all the way up to 10 days.

The map is based on distance from 8,518 cities with 50,000 or more people and only includes travel by land or water. The light areas represent places where travel to the city can be measured in hours rather than days. The major takeaway fact from this map is that the vast majority of people live in these lighter-shaded regions.

About 60 per cent of all cultivated land is within two hours of a city. In previous centuries those light zones would have been far fewer in number, but today's generation is able to take it for granted that the urban world is not so far away. Even if they live surrounded by fields and mountains, the city, with all its opportunities and problems, is a part of their ordinary lives.

Seen in this way, it's a map of a world in which the old distinction between rural and urban society is no longer useful. This erosion of rural-versus-urban differences isn't just true of the West. It is striking just how light India is on this map, as well as most parts of South America, East Asia and much of Africa. It is in these regions that, over the past fifty years, city expansion has been most aggressive. Not only have the great capitals expanded, but innumerable villages have become towns and towns have upsized to become cities.

Most of the darkest parts of this map are empty places. Hardly a soul lives in the bulk of Greenland, or the far north of Siberia and Canada; and the populations of the Sahara, the Amazon Basin or the Australian deserts, while not negligible, are very small. However, the map does point to a few remaining areas that have a sizeable population but which, in modern terms, are cut off. The Himalayas

53

Global urban population = 53% of the world

**60% of all
cultivated land**

2

hours travel

city

Nearly two-thirds of the world's
cultivated land is only two
hours' travel away from a city.

and the Tibetan plateau have a population that runs into the millions, though the
remoteness of at least some of this mountainous region is likely to lessen with
new road and rail routes that China is building. The dark zones in Indonesia –
West Papua and Borneo – may soon be among the few places left where a sizeable
group of people live far from any city.

CRITICALLY ENDANGERED
LANGUAGES

◉ Critically endangered

◉ Critically endangered – revitalised

◯ = One language

CRITICALLY ENDANGERED LANGUAGES

'After global warming, language loss is the earth's most acute crisis.' This bold statement by UNESCO reflects the scale and impact of the disappearance of so many of the world tongues.

There are 577 critically endangered languages shown on this map. They are the tip of the iceberg of language loss; the ones on the very edge of extinction. Calling them 'critically endangered' means they are confined to a last generation: the youngest speakers are grandparents or older, and they speak the language partially and infrequently. We can see how many of these languages lie in the Tropics: among indigenous groups in Amazonia, and among tribal communities in Africa and South East Asia. There are also many native languages in Mexico, the US, Canada and Australia that fall into this group.

Our data is derived from UNESCO's *Atlas of the World's Languages in Danger*. UNESCO has declared that of the more than 6,000 languages spoken across the planet, over 43 per cent are endangered, and that 'more than half of all languages will become extinct in the next 100 years at current rates'. They have launched an online interactive atlas that aims to keep track of the languages in danger. It is sadly indicative of the low priority given to the issue that this resource is underfunded. Languages that have evolved over thousands of years are disappearing and attempts to preserve or rejuvenate them are minimal.

The top ten languages in the world today account for about half of the world's population. This figure represents a dramatic shift towards language homogeneity. Increasingly people outside of this half want a stake in it, and look on their native languages as old-fashioned. About one hundred languages on the critically endangered list have only a handful of speakers left, such as Ainu in Japan and Yagán in Chile. Often having spent years being made to feel that their ancient tongue is a source of shame, the old folk who still know these languages mostly speak them only among themselves.

When the number of speakers drops really low, preservation efforts can get complicated. The last two surviving speakers of the pre-Columbian Mexican

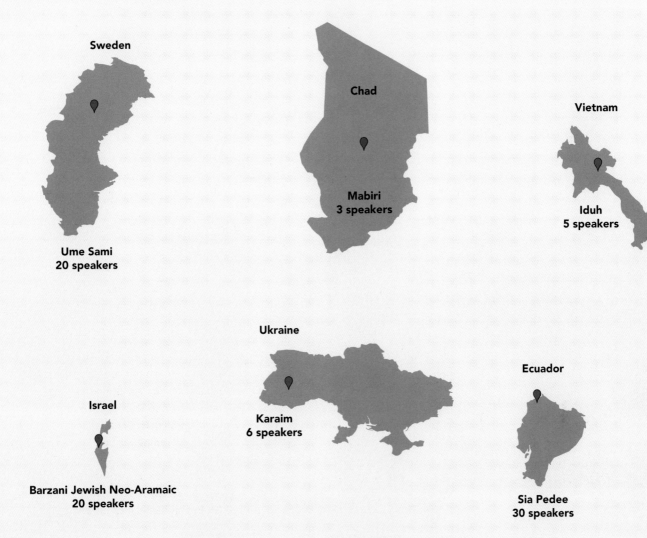

Sweden

**Ume Sami
20 speakers**

Chad

**Mabiri
3 speakers**

Vietnam

**Iduh
5 speakers**

Ukraine

**Karaim
6 speakers**

Israel

**Barzani Jewish Neo-Aramaic
20 speakers**

Ecuador

**Sia Pedee
30 speakers**

Mabiri is one of the most threatened languages in the world with an estimated three speakers left.

language of Ayapaneco didn't get on and refused to talk to each other. Moreover, such languages can wither even in the minds of those who once knew them well. Salikoko Mufwene, who is now a linguist at the University of Chicago, grew up in the Congo speaking Kiyansi, but found that when he went home after forty years away he was lost for words. 'I realised Kiyansi exists more in my imagination than in practice,' he says, adding, 'This is how languages die.'

Looking at the UK on the map, we see a couple of beacons of light. The last surviving native speaker of Manx, Ned Maddrell, died in 1974, and the last Cornish speaker, Dolly Pentreath, in 1777. But over recent years, small groups of activists have raised these languages from the dead. In future years, many more languages will need a similar resurrection.

WORLD NUT TRADE

- Almonds kernel
- Brazil Nuts kernel
- Cashews in shell
- Cashews kernel
- Hazelnuts kernel
- Macadamias kernel
- Pecans kernel
- Pine Nuts kernel
- Pistachios in shell
- Walnuts kernel

Width of arrow proportionate to
volume of trade

WORLD NUT TRADE

As world trade has become more global, there have been many attempts to create maps that show its flows and exchanges. Many are very specific, such as this simplified version of a map of the nut trade first published in 2015 by the International Nut and Dried Fruit Council Foundation. It shows us where the big production areas are, and the direction of import and export. At a glance it is apparent that production zones are very concentrated. The US dominance in almonds is clear from that large black arrow leaping from the US and heading for Europe. The statistics behind this one arrow are that, of the world total of almond kernels traded (464 tons; 472 tonnes), the great majority come from the US and, of these, 233 tons (237 tonnes) were exported to Europe.

Let's take another example: the large thick grey arrows coming out of West Africa. This colour denotes 'cashews in shell'. Of the world's trade total in this product (810 tons; 824 tonnes), West Africa sent 435 tons (442 tonnes) to India and 280 tons (285 tonnes) to Vietnam. This is a trade route between Africa and Asia; the former has the right environment for production, and the latter a food culture that uses a lot of cashews.

Some of the smaller centres of production are just as revealing. Turkey sends nearly all of its hazelnut kernels to Europe. Iran is a large source of 'pistachios in shell', and it sends them in every direction: of the world trade total of 135 tons (138 tonnes), Iran exports 32 tons (33 tonnes) to China, 19 tons (20 tonnes) to the United Arab Emirates and 14 tons (15 tonnes) to Europe.

There are other stories hidden in the smaller details. Looking at South America, we can see that Brazil nuts do not come from Brazil but from Bolivia, and that there's a smaller export from Peru. It turns out that the flowers of this huge nut tree are pollinated by tropical bees whose own reproductive cycle depends on their visiting a very particular orchid that grows high up in the tree canopy. That orchid doesn't grow in Brazil but it does grow in Bolivia and Peru. No orchid, no bees, no nuts; and so no purple arrows out of Brazil.

The cashew nut trade is dominated by the route from West Africa to Asia.

Simplified trade maps don't give us the full picture; like so many nuts, they need to be taken with a pinch of salt. Many of the smaller trade routes and sites of production aren't shown here, and the image we get is only as reliable as the data that is collected. However, as long we understand this, they are incredibly effective tools, enabling us to grasp quickly the state of play in a global market. The International Nut and Dried Fruit Council Foundation certainly seem to be feeling optimistic. They boast of a 56 per cent increase in tree nut consumption since 2004, and a 33 per cent rise in peanut consumption. Although their work appears more focused on the world of nuts than on dried fruit, they also note that we are eating more dried fruit, too, with large rises in production and consumption over the past two decades.

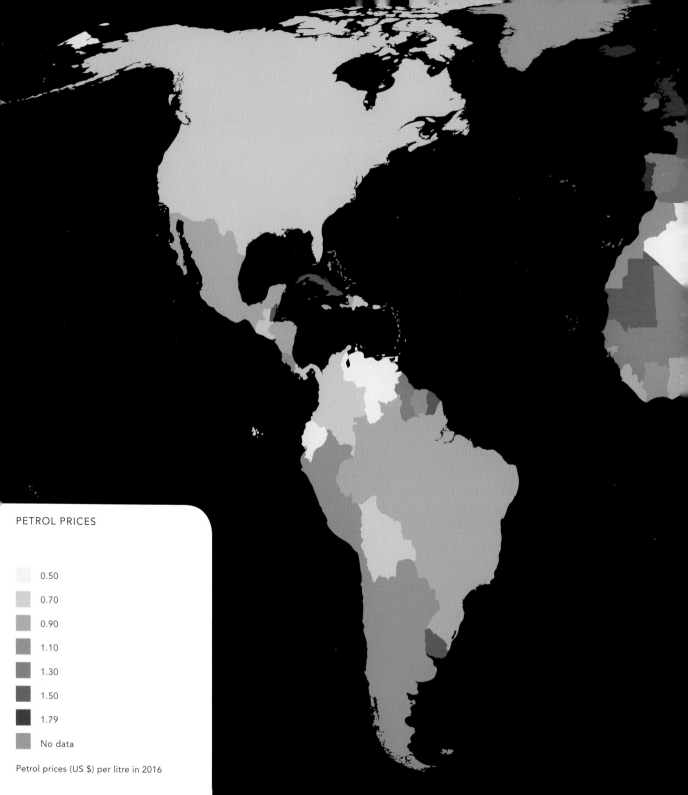

PETROL PRICES

	0.50
	0.70
	0.90
	1.10
	1.30
	1.50
	1.79
	No data

Petrol prices (US $) per litre in 2016

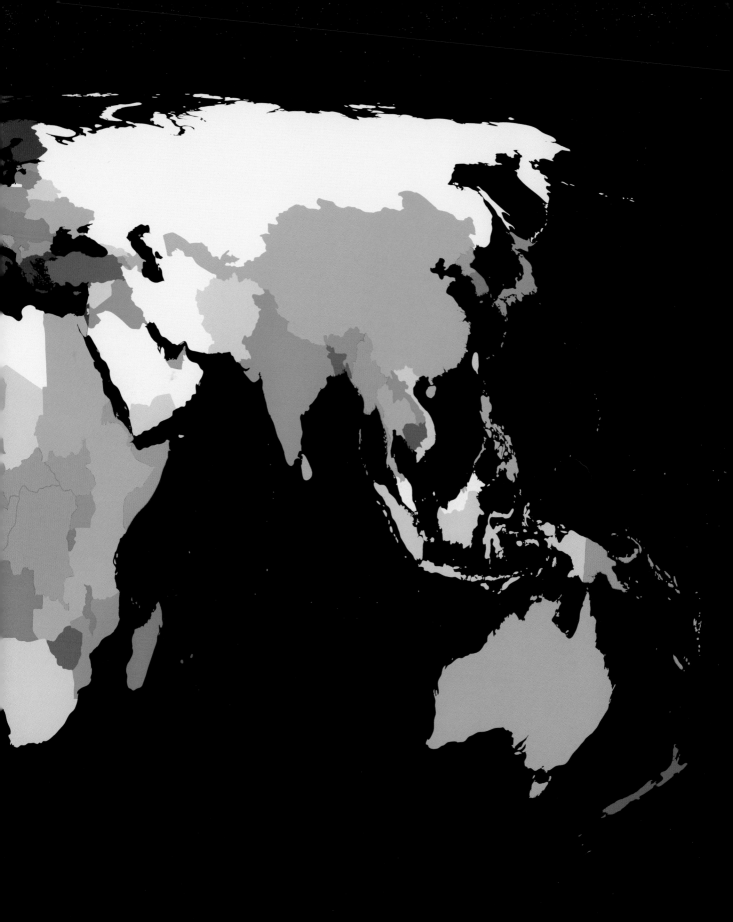

PETROL PRICES

Looking at this map, one understands why petrol-smuggling is such big business. The difference between petrol prices in Turkey and Iran, or Finland and Russia, is so large that it is bound to tempt people to import the stuff secretly or to nip across the border to fill up.

In Finland 'petrol tourists' take advantage of the fact that it is about half the price in Russia than in their own country. The high price of petrol across much of Africa might seem to be a bit of a puzzle; one would expect high costs in rich countries such as Finland, where large tariffs are applied and where most of the money goes to the government. But some of the world's steepest prices are in the poorest of places. The most deprived countries in Africa are often landlocked, necessitating high fuel transport costs. It has been estimated that 75 per cent of the fuel sold in Benin is smuggled in from Nigeria, where it costs half as much; and that smugglers from Togo and Burkina Faso get theirs from Ghana.

Government attitudes towards the issue are capricious. It is one of the easy levers that politicians pull either to increase revenue or become popular. In Angola, a big oil exporter, petrol used to be cheap, but the government decided to end this policy. Now it's very expensive, putting a stop to the lucrative smuggling trade that existed between Angola and its neighbours (the Central African countries tend to have very high petrol prices). Petrol is a basic commodity, and price hikes can get people out onto the streets and cause instability. In Nigeria in 2012 the new government tried to stop the subsidy on petrol and deregulate the price. A new, much higher price was announced. Nigeria is a big oil producer, and it appears that many people assumed this was just another way the government could squeeze them. A general strike was called and riots ensued. The government caved in and, as the map shows, now Nigeria enjoys a relatively cheap petrol price.

For many years, the country with the lowest price has been Venezuela. In 2014 petrol was $0.008 a litre. The government keeps the price very low, although in late 2018 they announced significant rises and in 2016 they allowed it to leap to $0.02. That's a big percentage increase, but a lot lower than in the US, where

Norway $1.62

Saudi Arabia $0.24

Italy $1.51

Algeria $0.21

UK $1.46

Venezuela $0.02

Three of the countries where petrol costs the most and three where it is cheapest.

drivers pay around 60 cents, or the UK, where a litre costs in the region of $1.50 or more. But national differences in petrol price aren't the end of the story. Fuel is cheaper in Colorado than in California; it costs much less in Adelaide than in Alice Springs. Petrol prices, are highly volatile and vary greatly from place to place, things that are unlikely to change in the coming years.

EDIBLE INSECTS

- 0
- 1–5
- 5–10
- 10–25
- 25–50
- 50–100
- 100–200
- 200–300
- >300

Number of edible insect species in zone

EDIBLE INSECTS

One of the last decade's more memorable headlines was: 'In 50 years we will all be eating insects'. If there is any truth to the idea, it's useful to look at where people are eating them right now. The map shows that it is a highly geographical habit; some countries eat a lot of varieties of insect, but a large group eat none or almost none. In some of the countries where it looks as if a diet of insects is common, like Australia, it is largely restricted to indigenous populations. A map of how many people eat insects would look rather different to this map, which points to the variety of insects that are eaten.

A few are well known: the agave worm, which feeds on agave plants, can be found resting at the bottom of tequila and mezcal bottles. In Mexico they are also eaten fried and sold in cans. Worldwide, crickets are the most common edible insect. There are 20,000 cricket farms in Thailand alone. They can be fried and roasted, and it's often said that they taste something like roast nuts, although having nibbled on a few I have to confess the pleasure was more in the crunch than the taste. Locusts, like crickets, are consumed across the insect-eating world. They are said to taste best when fed on sesame leaves.

There are a wide range of ants eaten in different places and in different ways. Leafcutter ants in Colombia and Brazil have been described as having a 'bacon-pistachio' flavour, while the more appetising-sounding lemon ants found in the Amazon are so named for their citrus notes.

The data for this map derives from a list of 2,040 edible insects compiled by Yde Jongema of Wageningen University in the Netherlands. His work shows that the largest group of insects eaten worldwide are beetles and weevils, and the next largest group are caterpillars.

Entomophagy, or insect-eating, is being touted as the next big eating phenomenon. A growing human population and the environmental toll of other forms of protein production, notably the amount of feed and land required for livestock, have turned people's attention to the potential of insects to feed the planet. They are protein-rich and contain many other micronutrients. They breed

15
Spiders

302
Ants, bees and wasps

35
Flies

634
Beetles

32
Cockroaches

359
Caterpillars

Numbers of the main different types of edible insect. There are far more varieties of edible beetle than any other insect.

easily and copiously and many are drought-resistant. Farming insects takes far less water than other types of animal farming. Insect farms take up very little land. Around 3.5lbs (1kg) of animal feed yields 12 times more cricket protein than beef protein.

What's not to like? Perhaps the answer to that question is rather obvious. Even in those countries where they are eaten, insects are more of a snack than a staple, and in those places where they aren't, the idea that we will be forced to eat them because the world is so crowded makes the prospect of a plate of fried beetles rather depressing. Advocates like to make the comparison with sushi, once thought outlandish in the West and now eaten everywhere. If we can be persuaded to eat raw fish, we can be persuaded to eat insects. I may be wrong, but I doubt it.

GUNS

<5

5–10

10–30

30–50

50–75

>75

No data

Number of privately owned guns per 100
residents, 2007 data

GUNS

The number of privately owned small firearms provides a good indication of the culture of gun ownership in a country. The darkest shades on the map indicate over 75 of this type of weapon per 100 residents. In the US there are about 80 guns for every 100 people, and since the population of the US is so large, that means 42 per cent of civilian-owned guns across the world are owned by Americans. These firearms are not evenly distributed. Three per cent of American adults are what might be called 'super-owners', having amassed around 17 guns per person.

Other areas with more modest but still relatively high gun ownership rates are the Arabian Peninsula (with Yemen standing out), a number of other countries in the Americas (notably Canada) and Northwestern Europe. Perhaps the latter is the biggest surprise on the map. Switzerland has gun laws almost as liberal as the US's. Although figures vary concerning the percentage of people who have a gun in Switzerland, it is conservatively thought to be about 25 per cent. France, Germany and the Scandinavian countries also hold a lot of guns, despite also having pretty tight gun laws.

In part the high numbers in Europe are explained by the number of people who are rifle-range and sport shooters, who collect or have inherited a weapon or who hunt. For example, in Germany there are about 300,000 people who collect guns, 900,000 who have inherited one, 1.5 million sport shooters and perhaps as many as 400,000 hunters. These are big numbers, and they suggest that firearms are not being acquired as offensive or defensive weapons but for other reasons; a fact that, in turn, helps explain why Germany has plenty of guns but little gun crime.

The large areas of low private-gun ownership in Africa and South and East Asia tell us that individual ownership of weapons is rare. We need to be careful about assuming this also means countries in these regions have little gun violence or even that they have fewer guns. In many places the majority of guns are in the hands of the army or militias. These guns can often be found in people's houses, but for the purposes of this map they haven't been counted. So, for example, in

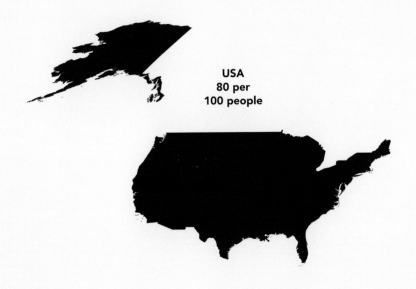

**USA
80 per
100 people**

**Yemen
54.8 per 100 people**

**Iceland
30.3 per 100 people**

**Germany
30.3 per 100 people**

Ratios of guns to people in two countries with little gun crime to two countries with a lot.

Israel lots of military personnel have government-owned guns in their homes — real weapons, but invisible in the figures on privately owned small firearms.

Sometimes the distinction between private and military use is hard to determine. Official figures tell us that Afghanistan has a rather low level of gun ownership. Yet there are plenty of news stories about the country being 'awash' with weapons, including many undocumented US weapons that have gone missing. Guns are often hard to keep track of. People keep them hidden and don't declare them. The world map of gun ownership tells us a lot, but it doesn't tell us everything.

PROBLEM DRUGS

Opiates

Cannabis

Cocaine type

Amphetamines

Others

No data

2009 data

PROBLEM DRUGS

One of the ways the continents divide themselves is in their drug habits. From Canada to Argentina the New World favours cocaine, no doubt because nearly all the world's supply of coca leaf comes from there (most of it from just three countries: Bolivia, Colombia and Peru). By contrast, across Europe and Asia the major problem drugs are opiates. There are, however, a few pockets of local colour: amphetamines in Saudi Araba and Japan; while Spain's links to South America find a reflection in its cocaine problem.

The map is based on the UN World Drug Report, which looked specifically at drugs in terms of 'treatment demand'. This means it's a reflection of which drugs are considered to be a medical and social problem as much as an indication of which drugs are actually being used. Admittedly it is a broad-brush report, and glosses over some big differences. One of these is that in North America the biggest problem drug is cocaine, but all three of the other drugs in the index are each responsible for between, very roughly, 20 per cent of drug treatment. Cocaine is much more dominant in Central and South America, and there is a far smaller problem with opiates.

Heroin is the most dangerous widely used opiate, and it is heroin use that explains the large patch of green across Asia and Europe. This dominance is in part a reflection of the fact that most of the world's illegal opium is grown in Asia, more specifically in Pakistan, Myanmar, Thailand and Afghanistan. The size of the problem caused by heroin is out of kilter with the actual number of people who take it, which different estimates put at between 9 million and 16 million people worldwide. This is a tiny number when compared to those who, for example, smoke cannabis, which is officially put at about 180 million but which is likely to be many more.

A general trend is the decline in drug use in the West, including the most dangerous and expensive drugs, such as cocaine and heroin, and their rise elsewhere, including in Africa's capitals. One of the surprising features of this map is that it points to a problem with cannabis in Africa. This is an under-reported

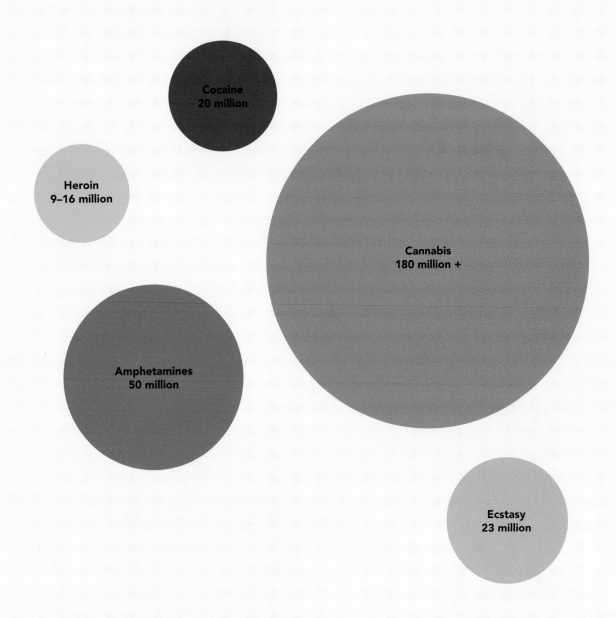

Cocaine
20 million

Heroin
9–16 million

Cannabis
180 million +

Amphetamines
50 million

Ecstasy
23 million

Number of drug users.
These official figures are
likely to be underestimates.

issue. Africa has the highest levels of cannabis production in the world, with the UN describing production on the continent as 'pervasive'. With moves towards the legalisation of cannabis in Africa, especially in South Africa, its status as a problem drug may diminish. Yet it is worth reminding ourselves that this is a map of treatments sought: hence it would be unwise to assume that cannabis will cease to be a problem drug just because it is legalised.

SUGAR CONSUMPTION

- <15
- 16–30
- 31–45
- 46–60
- 61–75
- 76–100
- >100
- No Data

Average grams per person per day

SUGAR CONSUMPTION

The world's sweet tooth is not equally shared. Across the Americas, Europe, Russia and much of the Middle East people love tucking into sugary foods. Much of Africa and East Asia doesn't have the same fondness for sweet things. That's not to say people there don't like sugar, but there are economic and cultural factors that stay their hand when pouring it in. A typical Russian or American will consume several times the amount of sugar per day than the average Chinese. It has been speculated that the amount of hot tea drunk in East Asia makes people more sensitive to sweet tastes and so less likely to keep adding it. Yet this map shows that hot-tea-drinking societies like Thailand also have a high sugar intake, so there must be other factors at work.

Sugar has traditionally been an expensive and unnecessary ingredient, so the poor have often gone without. As societies grow richer, tastes turn towards sweeter foods; sweetness and wealth have long gone hand in hand. Conversely, it's true that the more industrialised and processed food becomes, the more sweeteners get added to it because this is a cheap way of making it tastier. A lot of the sugar intake recorded on this map doesn't come in obvious forms, like bars of chocolate, but in packaged sauces, carbonated drinks and tinned foods.

This snapshot of sugar consumption may soon be out of date. In countries with a traditionally modest intake, tastes are changing. One of the big pressures on global cocoa supplies in recent years has come from the booming Chinese market. Chocolate sales in China have more than doubled over the past decade. At the moment, although the Asia-Pacific region contains over half of the world's population, it eats little more than 10 per cent of the world's chocolate. The average person in China gets through less than 5 per cent of the amount of chocolate an average Western European enjoys, but this doesn't look set to last.

Meanwhile, the health warnings about too much sugar being bad for you are curtailing consumption in the West. High sugar intake is linked to diabetes and obesity, and it is telling that this map was derived from work carried out by the World Dental Federation (based on data from the Food and Agriculture

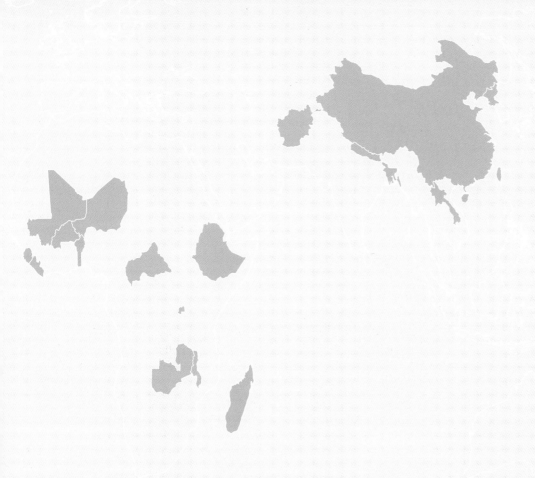

The nineteen countries
where people, on average,
consume less than 25g of
sugar per person per day.

Organisation of the United Nations). As people eat less sugar in some parts of the world, in others, like East Asia and Africa, they are eating more. The great geographical differences in sugar consumption which have survived into the twenty-first century may soon disappear.

MAP PROJECTIONS

An Uncommon Atlas includes four different map projections as well as a newer type of mapping, the chord diagram. We've mostly used Robinson or Eckert IV. Below are descriptions of the different projection types, and next to each map we list where these maps have been used.

Robinson: a world projection often used for thematic mapping. It is a compromise between an equal area and a conformal projection and is more distorted towards the poles.

Eckert IV: an equal area projection which distorts the scale along the Equator. Commonly used for educational and thematic mapping.

Gall Stereographic: this is a cylindrical projection with distortion increasing from 45° N and S towards the Poles. This projection is commonly used in world atlases.

Plate Carrée: this projection is used for simple world representations. The projection is equirectangular, where all lines of latitude and longitude cross at right angles.

ROBINSON

Asteroid strikes

Vulnerability to
natural disasters

Temperature anomalies

Precipitation change

Water stress

Nuclear energy and
renewables

Countries with the
largest number of
venomous animals

Neglected tropical diseases

Peacefulness

Bird diversity

Ecological footprint,
per capita

Linguistic diversity

Total fertility rate

Religious diversity

Obesity

Number of migrants

People living in the US
born outside the US

Remoteness from city

Guns

Problem drugs

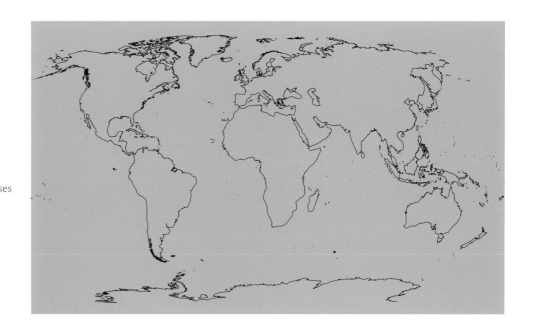

ECKERT IV

Rebounding land

Fire activity

Lightning

Amphibian diversity

Ants

Happiness

Critically endangered
languages

Petrol prices

Edible insects

Sugar consumption

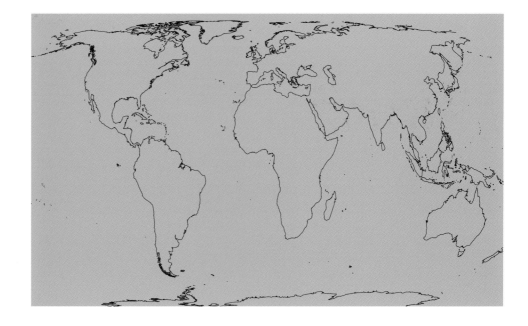

GALL STEREOGRAPHIC

Air pollution

Solar energy

Five per cent of the world's population

US fast-food franchises

World nut trade

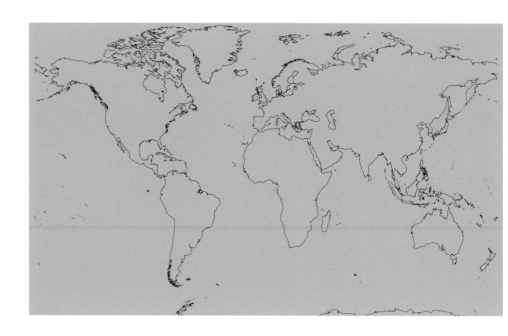

PLATE CARRÉE

Forests: loss and gain

Unknown oceans

Draining the oceans

Undersea cables

The Black Marble

Twitter relationships

Shipping routes

Energy flux

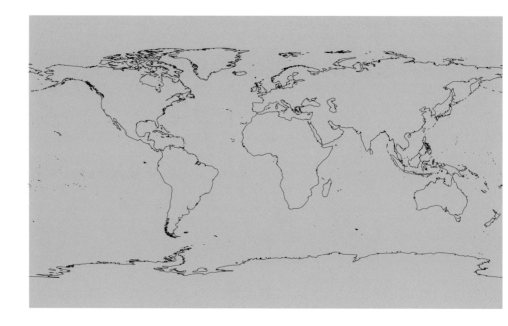

PLATE CARRÉE, PACIFIC CENTRED
Ocean rubbish
Sea level variations

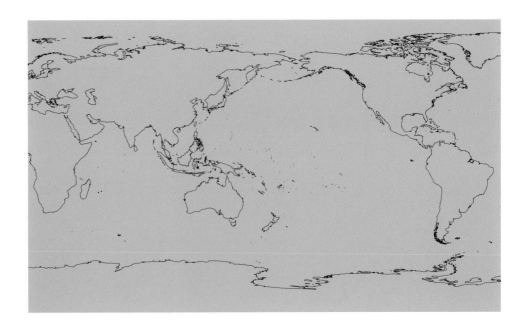

ECKERT IV, PACIFIC CENTRED
The unclaimed world
Drifters

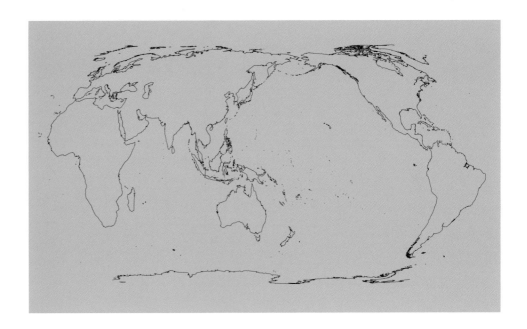

BIBLIOGRAPHY

Fire activity
NASA, Fire Information for Resource Management System, https://earthdata.nasa.gov/earth-observation-data

Asteroid strikes
NASA, Center for Near-Earth Object Studies, https://cneos.jpl.nasa.gov
[this site replaces the Near-Earth Object Program Office website]

Vulnerability to natural disasters
Alliance Development Works, United Nations University, The Nature Conservancy, *WorldRiskReport 2012*, Alliance Development Works, Berlin, 2012. http://reliefweb.int

Institut für Raumordnung und Entwicklungsplanung, World Risk Index, http://www.uni-stuttgart.de/ireus/Internationales/WorldRiskIndex [R]

Forests: loss and gain
Hansen, M. et al, *Global Forest Change*, University of Maryland: Department of Geographical Sciences, https://earthenginepartners.appspot.com

Water stress
World Resources Institute, Water Stress by Country, http://www.wri.org

Water: Mapping, Measuring, and Mitigating Global Water Challenges., http://www.wri.org/our-work/topics/water

Pangea Ultima
Scotese, Christopher R. "Research", *PALEOMAP project*, http://www.scotese.com

Rebounding land
Milne, G. and Shennan, I. 'Isostasy: Glaciation-Induced Sea-Level Change', *Encyclopaedia of Quaternary Science*, 2nd Edn, Elsevier, New York, 2013, pp. 452-259.

UNESCO, High Coast / Kvarken Archipelago, http://whc.unesco.org

Nuclear energy and renewables
REN21, http://www.ren21.net [R]

Air pollution
NASA, Measurement of Pollution in the Troposphere, https://terra.nasa.gov/about/terra-instruments/mopitt

Solar energy
World Energy Council, Solar, https://www.worldenergy.org [R]

Temperature anomalies
Lynch, P. and Perkins, L. 'Five-Year Global Temperature Anomalies from 1880 to 2016', *NASA* https://svs.gsfc.nasa.gov

Air traffic
Grandjean, M. *Connected World: Untangling the Air Traffic Network*, http://www.martingrandjean.ch

The unclaimed world
United Nations, 'United Nations Convention on the Law of the Sea', http://www.un.org/depts/los/convention_agreements

Ocean rubbish
Maximenko, N. and Hafner, J. *Marine Debris*, International Pacific Research Center, 2010, http://iprc.soest.hawaii.edu/news

NOAA Marine Debris Program, https://marinedebris.noaa.gov [R]

Unknown oceans
Census of Marine Life, http://www.coml.org

Draining the oceans
Mitchell, H. 'Draining the Oceans, *NASA*, https://svs.gsfc.nasa.gov

Drifters
NOAA AOML Physical Oceanography Division, The Global Drifter Program, http://www.aoml.noaa.gov

Lightning
NASA, Global Lightning Activity, https://earthobservatory.nasa.gov/IOTD

Undersea cables
TeleGeography, Submarine Cable Map, http://www.submarinecablemap.com

International Cable Protection Committee, https://www.iscpc.org

Sea level variations
Handleman, M. and Elkins, K. 'Earth's Rising Seas', *NASA*, https://svs.gsfc.nasa.gov

Precipitation change
European Centre for Medium-Range Weather Forecasts, http://www.ecmwf.int

Amphibian diversity
NatureServe, Global Amphibian Assessment: 2004-2014, http://www.natureserve.org/conservation-tools

Ants
Antsmap.org, GABI Visualization Tool, http://antmaps.org

Guénard, B. *The Global Ant Biodiversity Informatics Project*, https://benoitguenard.wordpress.com

Bird diversity
Biodiversitymapping.org, http://biodiversitymapping.org/wordpress

BirdLife International, Data Zone, http://datazone.birdlife.org

Countries with the largest number of venomous animals
Armed Forces Pest Management Board, 'Living Hazards Database', http://www.acq.osd.mil

Neglected tropical diseases
Centers for Disease Control and Prevention, Map: Global Overlap of Six of the Common NTDs, https://www.cdc.gov/globalhealth

Uniting to Combat Neglected Tropical Diseases, 'The London Declaration', http://unitingtocombatntds.org

Five per cent of the world's population
Galka, M. 'The Global Extremes of Population Density', *Metrocosm* http://metrocosm.com

Ecological footprint per capita
Henrie, G. 'World Ecological Footprint per Capita', *Situating the Global Environment*, http://dsarchive.lclark.io

Global Footprint Network, http://www.footprintnetwork.org [R]

Peacefulness
The Institute for Economics and Peace, Global Peace Index 2016, http://visionofhumanity.org

The Black Marble
NASA, Night Lights 2012 - The Black Marble, https://earthobservatory.nasa.gov/NaturalHazards

Carlowicz, M. 'Night Light Maps Open Up New Applications', *NASA*, https://earthobservatory.nasa.gov/NaturalHazards [R]

Linguistic diversity
Ethnologue: Languages of the World, https://www.ethnologue.com

Greenberg, J. 'The Measurement of Linguistic Diversity', *Language*, Vol. 32.1, Linguistic Society of America, Washington DC, 1956, pp. 109-115

Total fertility rate
CIA, Country Comparison: Total Fertility Rate, https://www.cia.gov/library/publications

United Nations, World Population Prospects 2015, https://esa.un.org

Religious diversity
Pew Research Centre, Global Religious Diversity, http://www.pewforum.org

Obesity
World Health Organisation, Prevalence of Obesity, Ages 18+, 2014 Both Sexes, http://gamapserver.who.int

World Obesity, http://www.worldobesity.org [R]

Happiness
Helliwell, J., Layard, R. and Sachs, J. *World Happiness Report 2015*, Sustainable Development Solutions Network, 2015, New York.

Royal Government of Bhutan, *The Report of the High-Level Meeting on Wellbeing and Happiness: Defining a New Economic Paradigm*, The Permanent Mission of the Kingdom of Bhutan to the United Nations, New York, 2012.

Twitter relationships
Leetaru, K. *et al*, 2013 Mapping the Global Twitter Heartbeat: The Geography of Twitter, *First Monday*, 18, 5, http://firstmonday.org

US fast-food franchises
The Data Team, 'Fast-food Nations', *The Economist*, 2015, http://www.economist.com/fastfood [R]

Daszkowski, D. 'The Expansion of American Fast Food Franchises', *the balance*, 2017, https://www.thebalance.com [R]

Shipping routes
Globaïa, The Global Transportation System, 2013, http://globaia.org

Anon., 'Free Exchange: The Humble Hero', *The Economist*, 2013, http://www.economist.com/news

Energy flux
Globaïa, A Cartography of the Anthropocene, http://globaia.org

Number of migrants
United Nations, International Migrant Stock 2015: Maps, http://www.un.org/en/development

Flow of people
Sander, N., Abel, G. and Bauer, R. *The Global Flow of People*, http://www.global-migration.info

Vienna Institute of Demography, http://www.oeaw.ac.at

People living in the US born outside the US
Pew Research Center, Origins and Destinations of the World's Migrants, from 1990-2015, http://www.pewglobal.org

Remoteness from city
Nelson, A. *Travel Time to Major Cities: A Global Map of Accessibility*, Office for Official Publications of the European Communities, Luxembourg, 2008, http://forobs.jrc.ec.europa.eu

Critically endangered languages
Moseley, C. *Atlas of the World's Languages in Danger*, UNESCO Publishing, Paris, 2010, http://www.unesco.org/culture

World nut trade
International Nut and Dried Fruit Council, 2014/2015 World Nuts & Dried Fruits Trade Map, http://www.nutfruit.org

Petrol prices
Emerson, K. 'Map of the Week: Oil Prices! See how the cost of oil has changed across the globe from 2014 to 2016', *American Geographical Society*, 2016, http://americangeo.org

Edible insects
Jongema, Y. 'List of Edible Insects of the World (April 1, 2017)', *Wageningen University & Research*, 2017, http://www.wur.nl

Guns
Small Arms Survey, http://www.smallarmssurvey.org

Geneva Graduate Institute of International Studies, Privately Owned Guns per 100 Residents, 2007, http://graduateinstitute.ch

Myers, J. 'This is What Gun Ownership Looks Like Around the World', *World Economic Forum*, 2016, https://www.weforum.org [R]

Problem drugs
Guardian Datablog, The World in Drugs Use 2009, *The Guardian*, 2009, https://www.theguardian.com/news

United Nations Office on Drugs and Crime, World Drug Report 2016, http://www.unodc.org [R]

Sugar consumption
World Dental Federation, *The Challenge of Oral Disease: A Call for Global Action: The Oral Health Atlas*, 2nd Ed., FDI World Dental Federation, Geneva, 2015, http://www.fdiworlddental.org

[R] indicates resource only

Afghanistan 143, 51, 205, 208
Amazon 12, 102, 106, 184, 188, 200
American Samoa 146
Angola 196
Antarctic 32, 36, 48, 52, 53, 60, 84
Antarctic Treaty (1959) 60
Anthropocene 168
Arabian Peninsula 20, 122, 150, 156, 204
Arctic 48, 52, 53, 61, 165
Arktika expedition (2007) 61
Armed Forces Pest Management, US 110
Asia 28, 32, 44, 56, 72, 80, 82, 92, 111, 114, 119, 123, 126, 130, 134, 138, 142, 146, 147, 150, 156, 160, 164, 165, 168, 172, 173, 176, 180, 184, 188, 192, 204, 208, 212, 213
Atlantic Ocean 48, 56, 64–5, 72, 76, 84, 89, 156, 164
Australia 12, 28, 32, 41, 44, 52, 60, 72, 76, 77, 84, 102, 110, 111, 130, 150, 160, 172, 181, 184, 188, 200
Australian Bureau of Meteorology 76
Austria 127, *127*
Air Pollution *42–3*, 44, 45, *45*
Air Traffic *54–5*, 56, 57, *57*
Amphibian Diversity *96–7*, 98, 99, *99*
Ants *100–1*, 102, 103, *103*
Asteroid Strikes *14–15*, 16, 17, *17*
Africa 12, 20, 24, 28, 29, 32, 40–1, 44, 48, 49, 56, 80, 92, 106, 142, 146, 150, 151, 156–7, 160, 164, 168, 172, 176, 177, 184, 188, 192, 193, 196, 204, 208–9, 209, 212, 213

Bangladesh 21, 84, 118, *119*
Bay of Bengal 118
Bhutan 127, 150
Bird Diversity *104–5*, 106, 107, *107*
BirdLife International 106
Birkmann, Professor Jörn 20
Black Marble, The *128–9*, 130, 131, *131*
Blue Nile 40
BMI 146
Bolivia 24, 192, 208
Borneo 102
box jellyfish 110
Brazil 24, 28, 41, *41*, 52, 98, 99, 107, 110, 111, 138, 151, 192, 200
Burkina Faso 196

California 88, 197
Canada 24, 36, 41, *41*, 61, 102, 111, 122, *123*, 146, 150, 168, 172, 180, 181, 184, 188, 204, 208
carbon monoxide *42–3*, 44, 45
Cartography of the Anthropocene 164
Census of Marine Life 68
Center for the Study of Global Christianity 142
Chelyabinsk, Russia 9
Chile 28, 60, 188
China 40, 45, 56, 60, 142, 156, 160, 165, 172, 180, 181, *181*, 185, 192, 212
climate change 21, 48, 92, 122
Colombia 110, 200, 208
Costa Rica 41, *41*, 127
Cuba 20, 134, 180, 181, *181*

Democratic Republic of Congo 40, 56, 57, *57*, 80

Denmark 60, 127, *127*, 150, 151
Desertification Research Centre, Spain 12
Deserts and Forests *22–3*, 24, 25, *25*
'desert power' 41
Dinoponera gigantea (ant) 102
Doggerland 72
Dominican Republic 180
Draining the Oceans *70–1*, 72, 73, *73*
Drifters *74–5*, 76, 77, *77*
drought 20, 28, 29, 52, 92, 201
Drugs, Problem *206–7*, 208, 209, *209*

Earth: shape of 37, *37*
Eastern Congo 80
Eckert IV map projection 214, 215, *215*, 217, *217*
Ecological Footprint Per Capita *120–1*, 122, 123, *123*
economic water scarcity 28
Economo, Evan 102
Edible Insects *198–9*, 200, 201, *201*
El Salvador 40, 106, 115
Energy Flux *166–7*, 168, 169, *169*
Ethiopia 115
Europe 24, 32, 36, 37, 41, 48, 52, 56, 92, 98, 111, 122, 126, 130, 134, 138, 146, 151, 156, 160, 164, 165, 168, 172, 173, 176, 177, 180, 192, 204, 208, 212
European Centre for Medium–Range Weather Forecasts 92

Fast Food Franchises, US *158–9*, 160, 161, *161*
Fertility Rate, Total *136–7*, 138, 139, *139*

Finland 24, 36, 40, 103, *151*, 196
Fire Activity 10–11, 12, 13, *13*
Five Per Cent of World's
    Population *116–17*, 118, 119,
    119
Flow of People *174–5*, 176, 177,
    177
'fore bulges' 37
Forests Loss and Gain *22–3*, 24, 25,
    25

Galka, Max 118, 119
Gall Stereographic map projection
    214, 216, *216*
GDP 126, 150
Geographic Cone Snail 110
Germany 151, 165, 173, 180, 204,
    205, *205*
Gibraltar 134
Gila monsters 110
Globaïa 168
Global Amphibian Assessment 98
Global Ant Biodiversity Informatics
    102
Global Drifter Program 76–7
Global Peace Index (GPI) 126–7
Global Trachoma Mapping Project
    115
globalisation 152–213
Great Pacific Garbage Patch 64–5
Greenberg, Joseph 134
Greenland 17, *17*, 36, 60, 81, *81*,
    119, *119*, 184
Guénard, Benoit 102
Gulf of Bothnia 36
Gulf States 56, 131, 176
Guns *202–3*, 204, 205, *205*
Gyres 64

habitat loss 98
Haiti 20, 134
Hansen, Matthew 24, 25
Happiness *148–9*, 150, 151, *151*
Henrie, Gabby 122
Himalayas 32, 48, 184–5
Hindi 134
Hong Kong 28, 102
human and animal 94–151
Hungary 40
Hussein, Saddam 130
hydropower 40, 41

Iceland 127, *127*, 151, *151*, 160,
    204, *204*
Indian Ocean 20, 164

Indonesia 28, 77, *77*, 110, 185
Insect Biodiversity and
    Biogeography Laboratory,
    University of Hong Kong 102
Institute for Economics and Peace
    126, 127
International Cable Protection
    Committee 85
International Nut and Dried Fruit
    Council Foundation 192, 193
Iran 192, 196
Iraq 127, 130, 172
Israel 127, 172, 189, *189*, 205
India 20, 28, 41, *41*, 48, 56, 84, 92,
    93, 110, 111, 118, 127, 134,
    135, 138, 139, 142, 164, 168,
    172, 180, 184, 192

Japan 21, 102, 146, 156, 168, 172,
    188
Jongema, Yde 200
Jordan 172

Kazakhstan 17, *17*, 172

Lake Maracaibo, Venezuela 80, *81*
Lake Victoria, Africa 106
land, air and sea 10–93
Languages, Critically Endangered
    186–7, 188, 189, *189*
Latin America 56, 114, 123, 150,
    157, 177
Lenin, Vladimir 130
Lesotho 41, *41*
Libya 138, 146
Lightning *78–9*, 80, 81, *81*
Linguistic Diversity *132–3*, 134,
    135, *135*
Living Hazards Database, The 110
London Declaration on Neglected
    Tropical Diseases 115

Mali 92
Map Projections 214–17, *215*, *216*,
    217
Mariana Trench 68, 72
Mawsynram, India 92–3, *93*
Maximenko, Nikolai 64
Measures of Pollution in the
    Troposphere (MOPITT) 44, 45
Mexico 28, 110, 111, 127, 150, 176,
    180, 181, *181*, 188, 200
Middle East 28, 29, 52, 126, 130,
    142, 146, 150, 168, 172, 212

Migrants, Number of *170–1*, 172,
    173, *173*
Morse, Samuel 82
Mufwene, Salikoko 189

NASA 44, 45, 53, 72, 88, 131
    Fire Information for Resource
        Management System 7
    Goddard Institute for Space
        Studies 52
    National Geophysical Data
        Center 72
    Near-Earth Object Observation
        Program 9
National Oceanic and Atmospheric
    Administration, US 76, 77, *77*
Natural Disasters, Vulnerability to
    18–19, 20, 21, *21*
NatureServe 106
New Zealand 41, *41*, 60, 122, *123*,
    127, *127*, 150, 172
Nigeria 138, 156, 157, *157*, 168,
    196
Nile 130, 131
North America 24, 36, 92, 122, 134,
    165, 172–3, *173*, *177*, 208
North Atlantic 48, 56, 64, 84, 89,
    164
North Korea 130, 134
North Sea 72, 130
Norway 40, 60, 122, *123*, 151, *151*,
    197, *197*
Nuclear Energy and Renewables
    38–9, 40, 41, *41*
Nut Trade, World *190–1*, 192, 193,
    193

Obesity *144–5*, 146, 147, *147*
oceans:
    Draining the Oceans *70–1*, 72,
        73, *73*
    Ocean Rubbish *62–3*, 64, 65, *65*
    Unknown Oceans *66–7*, 68, 69,
        69
Okinawa Institute of Science and
    Technology 102
Oman 172

Pacific Cartography 122
Pacific Ocean 20, 48, 64–5, *65*, 76,
    88–9, 110, 122, 146–7, 164,
    212, 217, *217*
Panama Canal 164
Pangea Ultima *30–1*, 32, 33, *33*

Papua New Guinea 72, 127, 134, 135, *135*, 143
Paraguay 40
Pausas, Juli 12–13
Peaceful Countries in the World, The Most *124–5*, 126, 127, *127*
People Living in the US Born Outside the US *178–9*, 180, 181, *181*
Peru 102, 173, 192, 208
Petrol Prices *194–5*, 196, 197, *197*
Pew Research Center 143, 181
Philippines 20, 21, *21*, 89, 180
Plate Carre map projection 214, 216, *216*, 217, *217*
Portugal 127, *127*
Precipitation Change *90–1*, 92, 93, *93*
Puerto Rico 180

Qatar 20, 56, *57*, 127

Rebounding Land *34–5*, 36, 37, *37*
Religious Diversity *140–1*, 142, 143, *143*
Remoteness From Cities *182–3*, 184, 185, *185*
Robinson map projection 214, 215, *215*
Russia 16, 24, 44, 61, 126, 130, 150, 172, 173, 196, 212

Sahara 12, 48, 49, 92, 184
Samoa 146–7
Saudi Arabia 20, 146, 172, 173, *197*
Schmidt, Gavin 52
Scotese, Dr Christopher 33
sea ice 52, 53, 89, *89*, 165, *165*
Sea Level Variations *86–7*, 88, 89, *89*
Shipping Routes *162–3*, 164, 165, *165*
Singapore 127, 143, *143*, *165*
Solar Energy *46–7*, 48, 49, *49*
solar power 40–1, 48–9
South America 24, 32, 40, 44, 48, 92, 98, 102, 106, 107, *107*, 110, 118, 126, 142, 156, 164, 172, 180, 184, 208
South East Asia 72, 84, 89, 92, 102, 106, 123, 134, 146, 147, 156, 160, 180, 188
South Korea 130, 134, 156, 180, *181*
Southern Ocean 89

Soviet Union 130
Speciation 98
Strait of Hormuz 164
Straits of Malacca 164
Sugar Consumption, Average *210–11*, 212, 213, *213*

Temperature Anomalies *50–1*, 52, 53, *53*
Thailand 200, 212
Tibetan Plateau 48, 185
Togo 196
Tonga 146
Tropical Diseases, Neglected *112–13*, 114, 115, *115*
Turkey 192, 196
Twitter Relationship *154–5*, 156, 157, *157*

UK 36, 48, 76, 52, 92, 127, 151, 156, 160, 189, 196–7
Ukraine 40, *189*
Unclaimed World, The *58–9*, 60, 61, *61*
Undersea Cables *82–3*, 84, 85, *85*
UNESCO 36, 188
Atlas of the World's Languages in Danger 188
United Arab Emirates 122, *123*, 150, 151, 160, 192
United Nations 139
   Convention on the Law of the Sea 60, 61
   High Level Meeting on Happiness and Well-Being 150
   World Drug Report 208
   World Risk Report (2012) 11
United States of America 99, *99*, *123*, 146, *157*
   Fast Food Franchises *158–9*, 160, 161, *161*
   People Living in the US Born Outside the US *178–9*, 180, 181, *181*
Unknown Oceans *66–7*, 68, 69, *69*
Vanuatu 20, *21*
Venomous Animals, Countries with Largest Number of *108–9*, 110, 111, *111*
Vienna Institute of Demography 177
Vietnam 110, 180, *181*, *189*, 192
Visible Infrared Imaging Radiometer Suite 131

Voluntary Observing Ship Program 76
Wagner, Tom 88
Water Stress *26–7*, 28, 29, *29*
West Papua 185
Wilson, Edward O. 103
World Dental Federation 212–13
World Happiness Report 150, 151, *151*
World Health Organisation (WHO) 114, 146
World Nut Trade *190–1*, 192, 193, *193*
Yemen 20, 84, 172, 204, *205*
Yeomans, Donald 16

CREDITS

10-11 J. G. Pausas and E. Ribeiro, 2013, Global Ecology and Biogeography; 13 Reto Stockli, NASA's Earth Observatory Team, using data courtesy the MODIS Land Science Team at NASA Goddard Space Flight Center; 14-15, 17 Planetary Defense Coordination Office, NASA Headquarters; 18-19, 21 © DW based on information provided by Bündnis Entwicklung Hilft, Berlin; 22-23, 25 © Hansen/UMD/Google/USGS/NASA; 26-27, 29 Gassert, F., P. Reig, T. Luo, and A. Maddocks. 2013. "Aqueduct country and river basin rankings: a weighted aggregation of spatially distinct hydrological indicators." Working paper. Washington, DC: World Resources Institute, November 2013. Licensed under CC BY 3.0; 30-31 © C. R. Scotese (U. Texas at Arlington), PALEOMAP; 33 Ziko-C / Public Domain; 34-35 Milne, G.A. and Shennan, I., 2013. Isostasy: Glaciation-Induced Sea-Level Change. In: S. Elias (Ed.), Encyclopedia of Quaternary Sciences (2nd edition). Elsevier, London, UK, pp. 452-459.; 37 © ESA/HPF/DLR; 38-39, 41 Maps on the Web http://mapsontheweb.zoom-maps.com/post/120939690653/percentage-of-electricity-produced-from-renewable; 42-43, 45 Abel, G. J., & Sander, N. (2014). Quantifying Global International Migration Flows. Science, 343(6178), 1520–1522. https://doi.org/10.1126/science.1248676; 46-47, 49 © Copyright 2014 All Rights Reserved - Natura Eco Energy Pvt. Ltd.; 50-51, 53 NASA/Goddard Space Flight Center Scientific Visualization Studio. Data provided by Robert B. Schmunk (NASA/GSFC GISS); 54-55, 57 Licensed under CC-BY-SA http://www.martingrandjean.ch/connected-world-air-traffic-network/; 58-59, 61 Licensed under CC BY-SA 3.0 cl; 62-63, 65 Nikolai Maximenko, International Pacific Research Center, School of Ocean and Earth Science and Technology, University of Hawaii; 66-67, 69 Ocean Biogeographic Information System. Intergovernmental Oceanographic Commission of UNESCO. www.iobis.org. Accessed: 2017-01-12.; 70-71, 73 NASA/Goddard Space Flight Center Scientific Visualization Studio U.S. Department of Commerce, National Oceanic and Atmospheric Administration, National Geophysical Data Center, 2006, 2-minute Gridded Global Relief Data (ETOPO2v2) - http://www.ngdc.noaa.gov/mgg/fliers/06mgg01.html; 74-75, 77 Drifting buoy data courtesy of NOAA's Global Drifter Program; 78-79, 81 NASA Earth Observatory image by Joshua Stevens using LIS/OTD data from the Global Hydrology and Climate Center Lightning Team; 82-83, 85 AIMS, GBRMPA, JCU, DSITIA, GA, UCSD, NASA, OSM, ESRI; 86-87 © Contains modified Copernicus Sentinel data (2016), processed by ESA and CNES; 89 © ESA/CNES/CLS; 90-91, 93 Image courtesy of Dr. Sean Birkel; 96-97, 99 AmphibiaWeb Copyright © 2000-2017 The Regents of the University of California; 100-101, 103 Janicki, J., Narula, N., Ziegler, M., Guénard, B. Economo, E.P. (2016) Visualizing and interacting with large-volume biodiversity data using client-server web-mapping applications: The design and implementation of antmaps.org. Ecological Informatics 32: 185-193.; 104-105, 107 BirdLife International and Handbook of the Birds of the World (2017) Bird species distribution maps of the world. Version 6.0. Available at http://datazone.birdlife.org/species/requestdis; 108-109, 111 Office of the Assistant Secretary of Defense for Energy, Installations and Environment (Armed Forces Pest Management Board) Living Hazards Database http://www.acq.osd.mil/eie/afpmb/livinghazards.html; 112-13, 115 U.S. Centers for Disease Control and Prevention; 116-17, 119 Original source http://io9.gizmodo.com/this-maps-red-and-blue-regions-each-contain-5-of-the-w-1719773481; 120-21, 123 Gabby Henrie, Lewis & Clark College Environmental Studies Program; 124-25, 127 Institute for Economics and Peace; 128-29, 131 NASA/Goddard Space Flight Center Scientific Visualization Studio U.S. Department of Commerce, National Oceanic and Atmospheric Administration, National Geophysical Data Center, 2006, 2-minute Gridded Global Relief Data (ETOPO2v2) - http://www.ngdc.noaa.gov/mgg/fliers/06mgg01.html The Blue Marble Next Generation data is courtesy of Reto Stockli (NASA/GSFC) and NASA's Earth Observatory. The Blue Marble data is courtesy of Reto Stockli (NASA/GSFC); 132-33, 135 Ethnologue 18 linguistic diversity index BlankMap-World6.svg. Licensed under CC-BY-SA 3.0; 136-37, 139 Data from CIA world factbook; 140-41, 143 Copyright 2016 Pew Research Center; 144-45, 147 data © World Health Organisation data © World Health Organisation Reprinted from http://apps.who.int/bmi/index.jsp?introPage=intro_3.html; 148-49, 151 Helliwell, John F., Richard Layard, and Jeffrey Sachs, eds. 2015. World Happiness Report 2015. New York: Sustainable Development Solutions Network; 154-55, 157 Image courtesy of Kalev Leetaru; 162-63, 165 NOAA's SEAS BBXX database, from 14.10.2004 to 15.10.2005; 166-67 National Geospatial-Intelligence Agency, September 2000; 169 FELIX PHARAND-DESCHENES, GLOBAIA/SCIENCE PHOTO LIBRARY; 170-71, 173 Licensed under CC-BY-SA http://www.un.org/en/development/desa/population/migration/data/estimates2/estimatesmaps.shtml?1t1; 175-76, 177 "The Global Flow of People" (www.global.migration.info) by Nikola Sander, Guy Abel & Ramon Bauer, published in Science in 2014 under the title "Quantifying global international migration flows"; 178-79, 181 United Nations Population Division; 182-83 © European Union, 1995-2017; 185 Created by David Marioni from the Noun Project; 185 Created by Yu Luck from the Noun Project; 186-87, 189 © 2016 – The Language Conservancy (this map is based on data from UNESCO & © UNESCO 1995-2010; 190-91, 193 INC International Nut and Dried Fruit Council; 194-95, 196 American Geographical Society © 2016. All Rights Reserved; 198-99, 201 Jongema, 2012; 202-203, 205 Licensed under CC1.0 Universal; 206-207, 209 Data from Mortality and Burden of Disease estimates for WHO member states in 2002; 210-11, 213 Food and Agriculture Organization of the United Nations, 2015, FDI World Dental Federation, "The Challenge of Oral Disease – A call for global action. The Oral Health Atlas. 2nd ed." http://www.nature.com/bdj/journal/v220/n9/full/sj.bdj.2016.322.html. Reproduced with permission.

ACKNOWLEDGEMENTS

This book has been a collaborative effort. Lucy Warburton at Aurum came up with the idea and has worked tirelessly on the project and Paileen Currie's excellent design has brought *An Uncommon Atlas* together beautifully. Thanks are due to the cartographers at Lovell Johns for making the maps and Jenny Page for correcting and editing the text. Also to Dr Wen Lin of Newcastle University for providing expert oversight and insight.

ABOUT THE AUTHOR

Alastair Bonnett is Professor of Social Geography at Newcastle University. His books have been widely translated and include *Beyond the Map*, *Off the Map*, *What is Geography?* and *How to Argue*. He has also contributed to history and current affairs magazines on a wide variety of topics, such as world population and the geography of nostalgia. Alastair lives in Newcastle.